THE ALTER EGO EFFECT

THE
ALTER
EGO
EFFECT

THE POWER OF SECRET IDENTITIES
TO TRANSFORM YOUR LIFE

TODD HERMAN

HARPER
BUSINESS

An Imprint of HarperCollinsPublishers

HarperCollins books may be purchased for educational, business, or sales promotional use. For information, please email the Special Markets Department at SPsales@harpercollins.com.

FIRST EDITION

Designed by Bonni Leon-Berman

Library of Congress Cataloging-in-Publication Data has been applied for.
ISBN 978-0-06-283863-6

20 21 22 23   LSC   10 9 8 7 6

For all the people who grew up in the middle of nowhere
(and Valerie, Molly, Sophie, and Charlie—go team!)

CONTENTS

PREFACE

BEFORE YOU ENTER

A NOTE FROM THE AUTHOR

The Alter Ego Effect was built to support ambitious people doing hard things. It's constructed to help you be more resilient, creative, optimistic, and courageous. I've had a sports science and peak performance training company for twenty-two years, and what you're about to unwrap is based not only on the work I've done with thousands of amateur, pro, and Olympic athletes, but also the art and science of how we work.

It's been shaped by the data collected from the more than seventy-five thousand business owners and professionals who have implemented this strategy. Their reports back about the wins, successes, and breakthroughs along with the tweaks and changes they've made have all been used to refine this strategy.

A final note: Since I started my practice and began working with more elite athletes, I made a commitment to privacy. I protect my clients. Some of the world's great Olympic and pro athletes as well as entertainers work with me because I promise never to use their names for personal benefit. Why? Because trust is the most essential currency I can trade. Everyone wants something from these people, they use them as a way to grab the spotlight, and it causes them to trust no one. I recognized it, and I knew it would prevent me from being the trusted advisor and coach they needed and wanted. I've worked with top business professionals as well, and the promise is the same. I hold that trust and promise sacred. But I also know how valuable and important it is to share their stories to help illustrate points and to make the ideas in *The Alter Ego Effect* spring to life for you.

Throughout the book, I have tried to balance the need to share my clients' stories with you, the reader, with my vow to my clients. To achieve this, I've sometimes changed details like names, a sport, an industry, and other identifying factors. In the end, these factors are actually irrelevant. As you're about to find out, the Alter Ego is a tool anyone, in any situation, in any profession, in any moment can use to bring forth their Heroic Self.

Todd Herman

THE ALTER EGO EFFECT

CHAPTER I

WHAT'S YOUR PHONE BOOTH MOMENT?

Standing in the greenroom looking at my notes, I waited to be called onstage before a crowd of coaches from the world of sports. As I was reviewing my presentation, a man built like a powerful bulldog walked into the room. I'd played him on Nintendo as a kid. He strolled over to me with a big smile, reached out, and said, "Hi, I'm Bo Jackson."

I laughed and said, "Hi, I'm Todd Herman. I know who you are, Bo. I'd probably lose all credibility if I worked in sports and didn't know the only two-sport all-star in the pros. Plus, you helped me win a lot of games on *Tecmo Bowl*!"

He chuckled and said, "Yeah, you're not the first to say that. And thanks. Are you speaking today, too?"

"Yeah. I'm up next. But maybe I just got bumped for you." I laughed.

"No, you're good. I just came early to see a friend," he said. "So what are you gonna talk about?"

"I'm going to talk about the mental game, but, specifically, I'm going to share with everyone how to use Alter Egos and Secret Identities to perform at your best."

Immediately, he cocked his head to the side slightly, squinted his eyes as if someone had just struck a deep chord inside him, and then smirked. He shook his head. After a few seconds, he said in a hushed, serious tone, "Bo Jackson never played a down of football in his entire life."

If you don't know Bo Jackson, he's the only athlete in the big four of major North American sports to be an all-star in two of them, Major League Baseball and the National Football League. He was a phenom who transcended sports in the 1980s and, for a sport-loving kid like me, a superhero.

My eyes widened as I smiled and said, "Ooookaayyy . . . interesting. Tell me more."

Bo went on to explain how as a youngster he had challenges containing his emotions and would get into a lot of trouble because of his anger. Often, he'd get caught up in the competition, and he'd retaliate against even the smallest perceived slights, causing him to get hit with unnecessary penalties.

One day, though, as he was watching a movie, he became fascinated by the unemotional, cold, and relentless nature of Jason. Does the name ring a bell?

Jason was the hockey mask–wearing killer in the *Friday the 13th* movies.

At that moment—during the movie—he resolved to stop being Bo Jackson and start being Jason on the football field, leaving the uncontrollable rage on the sidelines.

Bo went on to explain how Jason *only* lived on the field. And when he walked out of the locker room and reached the football field, Jason would enter his body and take over. Suddenly the hotheaded, penalty-prone, easy-to-provoke Bo Jackson transformed into a relentless, cold, and disciplined destroyer on the football field.

Channeling a "different" identity helped him focus every ounce of his talent and skill, and enabled him to show up on the field, without any emotional issues interfering with his performance.

It was his "phone booth moment." Just like Clark Kent would sometimes go into a phone booth to transform into Superman, Bo Jackson did the same thing when he transformed into his Alter Ego, Jason.

Except he didn't have to deal with annoying space issues like Superman explained in a 1942 comic: "This definitely isn't the most comfortable place in the world to switch garments, but I've got to change identities—and in a hurry!"

While it's a funny quote, there's something embedded in his statement that reveals the transformational nature of the Alter Ego Effect.

WHO'S THE ALTER EGO?

I've always been fascinated by comics, comic book heroes, and the worlds they live in. The origin stories, the villains, and the epic battles always found a way to draw me into their worlds. As a kid, I loved the Christopher Reeve Superman movies. Today people might laugh at those 1980s productions compared to the epic rebirth of superhero movies happening now, but back in the day, they were awesome. Now, here's a riddle for you:

Everyone knows that Superman and Clark Kent are the same. But which one is the alter ego?

I've asked this question for the past fifteen years, countless times in front of audiences around the world, and 90 percent of the audience immediately yell out, "SUPERMAN!"

It sounds right. Because when you think of "alter egos," you think of superpowers, heroism, and epic battles. All the qualities of a superhero like Superman.

Except—it's wrong.

The alter ego isn't Superman; it's Clark Kent. Superman is the real person. He created the alter ego, mild-mannered reporter Clark Kent, as a useful persona to go unnoticed day-to-day on earth and blend in to help him achieve a crucial goal: understanding humans.

Superman would flip between his alter ego and the S on his chest at precisely the moments when he needed each persona the most.

Why does this matter?

Because, frankly, life is hard. There are a lot of different responsibilities we all carry on our shoulders. There are a lot of different roles we play in life. And there are the constant forces of society—religion, families, teammates, coworkers, friends, and others—that lead us to act a certain way. These come in the form of expectations, rules, and judgments about how we're supposed to act. What we're allowed to pursue. What we should have. What we should believe.

All of this and more creates what I call the Trapped Self, which we'll reveal more of in chapter 3. This Trapped Self is the part of you that doesn't feel like it's showing up in life like you want, avoiding certain things or feeling pressured to act in a certain way.

Conversely, there's another experience we have in life, where we feel like our Heroic Self. It's that part of you that feels like you're doing what you want, doing it for your own reasons, and you get caught up in the flow of the activity. And it turns out there's fascinating research on the subject that explains the benefits of Alter Egos.

When you find yourself bored, anxious, angry, jealous, resistant, overwhelmed, or fearful, you can't reason yourself out of it. It's like a mouse trying to direct a herd of rampaging elephants. You can't logic your way out of an unconscious problem. If your gut is telling you to avoid it, you'll avoid it. But you can use that same unconscious power, tap into the mysteries of your imagination, and, with a little practice, change whose gut you're checking. And, lucky for us, research and science show us it's a better approach.

THE FIFTEEN-YEAR-OLD AND THE 4:35 A.M. TRAIN TO NEW YORK

Anthony was a basketball player at one of the best prep schools in the United States, with off-the-chart skills. During practice, he'd school

his teammates one-on-one. Scouts from all the top colleges were recruiting him, and people had him pegged as a possible pro baller one
day—IF. *If* he would show more poise during crunch time and believe
in his abilities more.

Anthony grew up in a low-income area of Washington, D.C., without a mom or dad. They both passed away in a car accident when he
was eight years old. His grandma took on the responsibility of raising
him and was doing a damn good job under the circumstances. As a
youngster, Anthony spent every second he could find taking refuge on
the basketball court, dribbling, shooting, and jumping.

He continued to develop, and soon scouts from all the top colleges
were recruiting him. People had him pegged as a possible pro-baller
one day—IF. *If* he would "get his head screwed on straight." For all of
Anthony's skills and abilities, there was just one problem. When the
game was on the line, instead of driving hard to the hoop or getting
the defender on his heels and then pulling up fast and firing a jump
shot, he'd pass the ball. He'd let a teammate take the shot, or choke.
And it was getting worse.

Anthony had all the skill in the world to seize the opportunity.
But he'd hide during what we call Moments of Impact, those critical
moments that define a large part of our success. For Anthony, he got
caught up in worrying about the criticism more than he wanted the
adulation. The more the spotlight was placed on Anthony, the more
he shrank from its glare.

It wasn't until his coach, in a fit of frustration, yelled at Anthony
during practice one day that he saw the answer. "Dammit, Anthony,
if you could only be more like James, we'd be unstoppable!" His mind
fired off a memory of an email he'd read once about athletes who used
Alter Egos on the court. When he got back home, he searched for the
email. Then he did the thing that would terrify any parent, let alone
his grandma.

At the age of fifteen, he snuck out of his house, went down to

Union Station in Washington, D.C., at 4 a.m., and caught the 4:35 Amtrak train to New York City.

In 2011, I spent most of my mornings working from the Reebok Sports Club on the Upper West Side of Manhattan. It was a beautiful club with six levels and every amenity you could imagine. It's also famous for being a celebrity haven, because they'd be left alone to work out, people like Chris Rock, Regis Philbin, Dwayne Johnson, Will Smith, Diane Sawyer, Ben Stiller, and many others. It was also where NBA teams would come and practice before games at Madison Square Garden. I had a routine of always arriving at around 8:45 and working in the private cafe for members. Then I'd get in a workout before lunch.

One day, as I walked into the lobby area, the front desk staff waved me over as soon as I got out of the elevators. They told me that the young man sitting over in the waiting area had come all the way up from D.C. to see me this morning. They said, "He came up here to see you and get help with his game. This freakin' kid is dedicated!"

I walked over to Anthony and introduced myself, while he jumped out of his chair to shake my hand. "Mr. Herman, it's a pleasure to meet you. I hope I'm not being a problem, but I need your help."

I brought him into the cafe, where we grabbed some breakfast and sat down at a table. I asked him, "First, how the heck did you know to come here? Second, do your parents know you're here?"

"You mentioned it in one of your email newsletters," he said, "that you come here in the mornings, so I thought I'd take a shot. And, no, my grandma doesn't know. I snuck out of the house at 4 a.m., but she wouldn't know anyway, because I leave early in the morning for school before she's up."

"Okay, well, first things first, you need to call your grandma and let her know where you're at and that you're safe."

After we got through the logistics of his escape from D.C. and I re-assured his grandma I'd make sure he got home safe, we talked about his situation. He explained what was going on and that the more pressure he was feeling and the more people were watching him, the more he was overthinking things. He talked about the anxiety and how he felt, saying, "There's a war going on in my head.

"I *really* want this, but I'm so worried about what everyone thinks of me and making a mistake."

Now, I'm not a therapist. I don't do therapy, and I'm terribly unqualified to do that kind of work. I work on the mental game and developing strategies for high performance. However, there's a simple framework I always use to diagnose the root of someone's problem, which I'll walk you through in chapter 3. It didn't take long to figure out Anthony's issue.

"So why did you come all the way up to New York, just to see me?" I asked.

"Because Coach said something to me that made me remember one of your emails about the sidelines of life. And how many great athletes use Alter Egos to help them perform better and leave parts of themselves on the sidelines. Because sometimes parts of their personality could be hurting their performance. And when Coach told me to 'be more like James,' I thought of you."

"Well, that's great, but why didn't you email me, instead of stressing out your grandma?"

"You always say, if you want something, go get it. And if you want something faster, go get it with a great mentor. I remember you talked about how you traveled all the way from Canada to North Carolina to meet a mentor once to spend weeks with him and that it was one of the pivotal moments of your life. So I thought, I should do the same. But just so you know, I don't have any money to pay you."

I fell in love with this kid. Chris Rock even stopped to give him words of encouragement when he was waiting for me. The staff told Chris what he'd done.

Over the next couple of hours, I peeled back the onion on his game, and it was apparent that the spotlight he was shunning had nothing to do with the court. It had everything to do with the pain he'd felt when his parents passed away. In the aftermath, he'd had different people showering him with attention, even fighting over who should have him and the insurance money. All he'd wanted was to be left alone.

Now the spotlight was back on, and Anthony was feeling the same thing all over again.

Like I said, I don't do therapy, and I wasn't about to start. I suggested he talk to his school counselors or grandma about getting some help, because "a great therapist can help unravel the fried wires in your head. But for now, let's leave Anthony on the sidelines and create an Alter Ego you can take on the court and get back to dominating."

I walked Anthony through the process of creating his Alter Ego for his Field of Play, the basketball court. And when we got to the point of unpacking the people, characters, things, or animals he'd love to embody, he said, "A black panther. They come out of nowhere, they're quick to strike, and they're fluid. I watched this National Geographic show on them once, and the way they moved was just so cool. Plus, they can jump twenty feet! And they have this cool name, 'ghost of the forest.'"

Watching him describe his Alter Ego—hell, I got excited. The next step was to give his Alter Ego a name. We brainstormed a bunch of different names in my notebook:

- The Black Panther
- Panther X
- Anthony Stealth

Nothing was popping for him until I suggested a name that made him come alive, "the Black Ghost." I'll never forget. The kid sat back in his chair, raised his hands behind his head, looked up, and said, "I *am* the Black Ghost, and I'm going to bring Mom and Dad onto the court with me and haunt everyone."

What Anthony did was something profound, and what I want to help you do, too, throughout the book. I left out of Anthony's transformation something crucial to building an Alter Ego that works for you.

Now, whether you have some old trauma that's somehow interfering with your desires, or you've told yourself a story about what you can or can't do, or there's some undefined resistance holding you back from pursuing something, I want to tell you there's a Heroic Self waiting to get unlocked, and that an Alter Ego or Secret Identity is the key to Activating it.

When you see how an Alter Ego fits into the human condition, the different roles we play in life, and the Fields of Play we stand on, it gives you the freedom to unlock a creative force. When you see how an Alter Ego helps you battle the natural challenges we all face with greater optimism, it can unlock a more playful and empowering approach to overcoming fear. And when you see it's a natural part of being human, has been used by tens of thousands of people to achieve goals both big or small, and is the most "real you" you could be—it will unlock hidden capabilities you didn't know were there.

Before I go any further, I need to make a quick disclaimer, because I don't want to mislead you with that last paragraph.

This isn't a motivational rah-rah book filled with cotton-candy ideas plucked from other cotton-candy self-help books that riddle the bookshelf and e-readers. This isn't a book with an "easy button" buried inside it. There is no treasure map to a pile of gold coins.

This book is for real people doing hard things. This isn't a book to remove the challenge of life. It's to take the part of you that shows up when you least expect it, and show you how to get it to show up when you most need it.

Your imagination can build Extraordinary Worlds and Ordinary Worlds. You've already been doing this. And here's a reminder that playfulness doesn't stop at eight years of age; it's a pathway to handling life with more grace.

Bottom line one: If you've got ambition, welcome to the tribe.

Bottom line two: If you're someone who wants to argue for your limitations, wait until everything is "perfect," or cowardly troll the ambitions of others, well . . . I'll leave you to decide what to do.

THE FINAL GOAL

I've devoted the last two decades to answering one simple question: How can I help the ambitious people I serve take the capabilities already nested inside and use them to perform at peak levels, consistently? Having built a peak performance and sports science practice over the past two decades, and coaching some of the world's Olympic and professional athletes, top business leaders, entrepreneurs, and entertainers, I've been faced with situations like:

How do I help the pro tennis star win championships instead
   of losing matches because she lets her opponents come from
   behind?
How do I help the Major League Baseball pitcher stand on the
   mound before a crowd of forty thousand screaming fans and
   lead his team to a playoff victory instead of choking and letting
   batters knock him around?
How do I get the sales executive to close more deals so his
   company grows and he gets promoted?
How do I help the entrepreneur proudly market her services
   instead of letting her new venture barely scrape by?
How do I help the hard-charging manager or VP become a
   calmer, more controlled, and better leader or coach with direct
   reports?

How do I help the parent struggling to juggle the demands of life and work be more attentive, loving, and fun at home?

How do I help the Broadway star slip into her flow state faster instead of feeling the terror and nerves of performing before live audiences?

The answer to those questions was and is an Alter Ego.

Back in the greenroom, Bo and I talked about the concept of Alter Egos, the other athletes using them, the process I'd use with clients, and that people in business and everyday life used them to achieve various things. For Bo, creating an Alter Ego was something he stumbled on naturally. He thought he was the only one to use it.

For decades we've been ignoring the bread crumbs and signs from history that the Alter Ego is a natural part of the human condition, and this book is about changing that.

I've waited fifteen years to write *The Alter Ego Effect*, and my goal is to teach you the same method I've taught my clients for almost twenty years, so you can use one or many to overcome feats both big and small. I'm going to show you how to Activate your Heroic Self—your inner Wonder Woman, Dalai Lama, Black Panther, Oprah, or Mr. Rogers—drawing forth the full range of your capabilities, skills, beliefs, and traits, so you see what you're *truly* made of. I'm also going to share with you the science behind why this method is so effective and share the stories of Olympians, business professionals, moms, entertainers, authors, children, and myself, who have all used it to overcome challenges.

I used it and use it still, and there's a reason why a pair of glasses is on the cover . . . but whose are they?

CHAPTER 2

THE ORIGIN OF ALTER EGOS

Shep Gordon is known as the *Supermensch*. He's a talent manager, Hollywood film agent, and producer. *GQ* called him the "Unfamous Man Who Made Everyone Famous." Shep played a pivotal role in the careers of Jimi Hendrix, Alice Cooper, Teddy Pendergrass, Luther Vandross, Raquel Welch, and Groucho Marx. Shep is what you could call "old-school." He never has contracts with his clients. Everything is done with a handshake and everyone "in the biz" knows: if he says it will happen, it will happen.

Shep is the person responsible for the celebrity chef world we live in today—he literally invented the market. Emeril Lagasse, Daniel Boulud, Wolfgang Puck, and more would be unknown to the general public if it weren't for Shep. Actor and director Mike Myers even produced a documentary on his life, aptly titled *Supermensch: The Legend of Shep Gordon*.

I happened to meet Shep at one of the world's premier events for creators, entrepreneurs, and artists, Mastermind Talks, hosted by Jayson Gaignard. Shep is one of the greatest storytellers you could ever meet. His stories about Alice Cooper are both rich and hilarious, though it doesn't hurt that he has some of the most iconic material to work with.

While I was sitting in the audience of 150 people, listening to Shep recount his tales as a scrappy Hollywood superagent, someone asked him how he helped the "high performers" he worked with "find that extra gear" and continue to perform at a high level.

Shep Gordon's response was honest, poignant, and profound:

> I think each one is very, very different. I think there's just one general rule that I used to try and give to every artist, whether they were chefs or they were entertainers. It's that if you allow the public figure to actually be you, you're never going to be happy. And you're never going to be confident, because if you take the traits of who you are and develop that into a character that you understand, you'll always know what that character should do, so when you're in a press conference, you always know how to answer a question.
>
> If it's you personally, you never have the answers. It's really tough, and when you take it personally, that's when you start scarring. If a bad review is about that person, you change that person. If a bad review is about you, sometimes that wound can be very deep. So, I don't think you can generalize, but if there's any generality, I would say, it's if someone who's in the public eye can understand that people aren't loving you, they're loving that character that's been put in front of them. Even from my movie, I get people come up to me, "You're the greatest. You're unbelievable." They don't know me. They know that guy. So, if you can keep that distance in your own brain, it's much healthier.

About fifteen people in the audience who knew my work looked over at me immediately. Some had dropped their jaws in amazement. Some grinned and winked. And Jayson, conducting the interview from the stage, found me in the crowd and shook his head with an "OMG, you've been talking about this forever!" look in his eyes.

(If you'd like to watch the clip, go to AlterEgoEffect.com/shep.)

Afterward, Shep and I discussed the concept more and how it was something far more universal than just a celebrity, entertainer, or athlete using it while under the spotlight of a stage or field.

An Alter Ego is a useful tool to help you, me, and others handle the adversity of life with more resiliency. Explore our creative sides, while protecting a fragile self. Be far more intentional about who we're trying to be on the Fields of Play. It's not only backed by the thousands of people who have used Alter Egos, but, more specifically, the system I've created over the past two decades is also backed by research and the success stories of numerous people you'll read about in the chapters to come.

THE ROOTS

The first-century BC Roman statesman and philosopher Cicero was the first documented person to talk about the Alter Ego, in his philosophical works, although the term he used was "a second self, a trusted friend."[1]

Its actual Latin meaning is "the other I."

These are all important distinctions because the concept has been around for centuries. And when you look at the roots from which the idea was shared, "trusted friend" or "the other I," they're extremely healthy terms. And if Cicero were alive today, he'd admit he was simply giving form to a naturally occurring part of the human condition. Just as I didn't invent Alter Egos, Cicero didn't, either. The only thing I've done is create a system for building one and give you a framework to activate its tremendous benefits, the Alter Ego Effect. And you'll see throughout the book the way people have used it for any number of purposes.

I first stumbled onto the power of Alter Egos as a teenager, growing up on a six-thousand-acre ranch in a small farming community in Alberta, Canada. I was an outgoing, ultracompetitive, and sports-loving kid. I would challenge my older brothers, Ross and Ryan, to anything. I'd lose most of the time, but I knew that *someday* I'd be able to beat them, and that when it happened, I'd never let them hear the end of it.

Sports were my refuge. Because underneath the cocky, competitive kid was a terribly insecure and worrisome kid. My mind was always rolling over whether people liked me, how to win people over, or how to impress them. When I played sports, all of that went away and my competitive spirit took over.

There was just one catch: I couldn't control my emotions.

When I was fourteen, my tiny rural school of Schuler was playing in a volleyball tournament in Golden Prairie, Saskatchewan. During the tournament, a player across the net was driving me nuts. Every time he went to spike the ball or jump for a block, he purposely kicked out his foot, trying to kick me in the groin.

The first time, I let it slide, because I thought it was an accident. But he kept at it. I complained to the refs, but it was obvious they weren't going to call a foul on the home team. As the game went on he started getting more and more brash. Finally, after a solid kick to my groin, I erupted. When his feet touched the ground, I reached through the net, grabbed his shirt, pulled him in, cocked my fist like a loaded pistol, and smashed him in the face through the net. He crumpled.

The place went crazy. Or about as crazy as a junior high volleyball tournament can get. Whistles started blowing, players and coaches rushed the floor, and my teammates looked at me like, What the hell just happened?

Later that day—after I'd been thrown out of the tournament—my coach, Mr. Henderson, sat me down for a heart-to-heart. He reamed me out for fighting and for making the school look bad.

He had wanted to talk to me for a while about my sportsmanship, but a good ol' fight finally tipped the can. He told me I needed to drastically overhaul my attitude. Mr. Henderson knew I had aspirations to play college football one day, but he told me, "Todd, you're hard to coach because you're a know-it-all. Nobody likes playing with you, because you just yell at them for mistakes. And unless you turn things around, you're going to make it a lot harder than you need to, to get to where you want to go."

Mr. Henderson was one of many mentors I've had in life. Some could read that and think he was being harsh. We were close and I respected him. But that didn't mean I didn't argue back. Because I did.

Like any great coach, he didn't leave me in a place to figure it out on my own. "If you want to achieve the goals you have, then you need to master what's happening inside of you," he told me. "When you get to school on Monday there's a book in the library I want you to get and read."

I did as I was told and Monday I grabbed the book from the library. Frankly, it was terrible. However, there was one good thing that came out of it, and it was something the author mentioned regarding the mind. It tapped into my curiosity to learn more, and I began to study the inner game, mental toughness, meditation (which back then was still pretty "woo woo"), and how to get into the zone.

ANOTHER VERSION OF ME

Back in 1877, legendary Native American chief Sitting Bull fled across the border into Canada after the Battle of the Little Bighorn and the death of Colonel George Armstrong Custer. When the natives entered Canada, they were met by Royal Canadian Mounted Police and granted refuge from the U.S. Army. Sitting Bull stayed in the area for four years, brokering peace deals with other tribes until finally returning to the United States and surrendering. My family's farm isn't far from where they entered Canada and where they ultimately hunted, gathered, and lived.

While this has nothing to do with volleyball outbursts, it does have a lot to do with the rest of this book and helping you find a source of inspiration to unlock a Heroic Self.

Growing up on the farm and doing whatever job Dad needed us to do meant we were constantly digging, pulling, and navigating the large swath of open prairie. While out on our tasks for the day, we'd come across old "fire rings," places where natives camped for the night, and I'd always dig around them to see if I could find any arrowheads or other artifacts.

Because of the rich history of the area, I became extremely interested in Native American culture. One day while lying on the sofa reading up on war dances, a ceremony where a small group of natives would dance around a fire ring, chanting, I learned the purpose was to "gather as one" and channel the spirits to help them in their quest.

Suddenly it clicked. I put the book down on my chest and visualized channeling a tribe of warriors to take out onto the field with me. I felt supported, focused, and depended upon. The idea gave me an incredible sense of calm and purpose.

The next time I stepped onto the football field, I went out as a tribe of warriors. I was a scrawny but fast little kid, and I wanted to play with more power. It seemed to help keep me focused, but I wanted something more. So, I thought about channeling players I admired, people like Walter Payton, the phenomenal running back for the Chicago Bears, and Ronnie Lott, the devastating defensive player for the San Francisco 49ers. Before football games, I would take five of Payton's and Lott's trading cards and strategically slip them into my uniform. I would put one of Payton's cards inside my helmet, and one on each of my thigh pads, imagining that I would run and see the field just like him. Then I would take Lott's trading cards and slip one into each shoulder pad, imagining that I could unleash devastating hits and tackles just like he did. I taped everything down and would go on the field as my Frankenstein-like Alter Ego. It was patched together from a few different sources, but it worked.

As a result, I played way bigger than my scrawny size. In the end, I reached my goal and played college football.

It didn't solve all my problems by any stretch, because I still dealt with problems at school and in my personal life, but on that Field of Play I left those problems on the sidelines and stepped into the best version of myself so I could compete. Like Shep mentioned, the Alter Ego became a shield for my Core Self and gave me a clear image of who needed to perform on that field to win.

THE MYSTERIES OF THE MIND

Beloved British actor Rowan Atkinson, famous for his character "Mr. Bean," was bullied for his stuttering throughout his school years.

As he progressed through school and eventually earned an MSc in electrical engineering from Oxford University, he discovered something profound. While in school, the boy who overarticulated and stuttered developed an interest in the dramatic arts.

In the August 23, 2007, issue of *Time* magazine, Atkinson was asked if he still stuttered. He simply replied, "It comes and goes. I find when I play a character other than myself, the stammering disappears. That may have been some of the inspiration for pursuing the career I did."

Atkinson's experience highlights a fascinating aspect of the human condition: we don't know everything there is to know about how the brain works. We're still working on mapping the "undiscovered country." However, we do know that our imaginations are an incredible force to create new worlds and new possibilities if used with intention. In other stories I'll share, athletes have altered aspects of their physical performance by tapping into "another self." This has happened despite the fact their parents had spent thousands of dollars on skill training that couldn't fix the problems. It's a mystery of the mind . . . but there are some theories on why it happens.

DIFFERENT PLACE. DIFFERENT TIME. SAME METHOD. AND JONI JACQUES.

Flash forward to my early twenties, and I again returned to this concept of the Alter Ego, although that wasn't what I called it at the time. I had just started a sports training business in my spare time. I was having success through the referrals I was getting, but it wasn't enough to sustain it. I knew I could help people, but to actually get out there and market myself tied me up inside. I was insecure about how young I was and worried no one would take me seriously. After all, you need to be at least forty to be taken seriously. (That was actually a rule I had in my head, that forty equals respect. Don't ask me how it got there, because it was absurd.) It didn't help that I thought I looked like I was twelve.

One afternoon, while I was "self-suppressing," which means avoiding doing the work I was supposed to, I watched an episode of *Oprah* that changed my life. That last sentence is a cliché, but clichés are clichés because they're true. It was 1997 and Joni Jacques shared with the audience how she had purchased a pair of Oprah's shoes during a charity sale, and it changed her life. She said, "I bought the shoes, and I really loved them, and I kept them in my bedroom. And when I got really, really depressed, and I couldn't find anybody to talk to, I took the shoes out and—"[2]

Oprah cut in, "Stood in my shoes. She would stand in my shoes, and now she says she doesn't have to stand in the shoes as much because she's standing on her own."

Later Joni shared that "the weight of the world just dropped off. Life totally changed that day."

A lightbulb went off at that moment, and I remembered the Alter Ego I'd use on the sports field. Joni had made something pop. For some reason, it hadn't occurred to me to use it in business, but in the end, that world was just another field to perform on.

Just as Joni used a pair of shoes to feel more confident, I knew immediately what I was going to use to step into a better version of myself in business. Growing up, all the smart people I knew wore glasses. When we're young, we establish beliefs and attitudes about the world around us that shape our thoughts and behaviors. I had come to equate being taken seriously and being smart with wearing glasses.

So I thought, What if I wore glasses? I figured—as absurd as it sounds—it was worth a try. I thought people looked smart and serious while wearing glasses, so perhaps prospective clients would think so, too. In fact, a variety of studies have found that people wearing glasses are perceived as honest, industrious, smarter, and more dependable.[3] Even defense lawyers ask their clients to wear glasses at trial. Lawyer Harvey Slovis explained to *New York* magazine: "Glasses soften their appearance so that they don't look capable of committing a crime. I've tried cases where there's been a tremendous amount of evidence, but my client wore glasses and got acquitted. The glasses create a kind of unspoken nerd defense."[4]

It also turns out one of the most respected men of the twentieth century and a leader of millions wore glasses when he didn't need to.

Martin Luther King Jr. wore glasses because he felt they "made him look more distinguished."[5]

The glasses on the cover of this book look a little like Clark Kent's, and a little like mine. However, to me, those glasses are Dr. King's. They're meant to be a signal and reminder that Great People have used elements of this concept with purpose, and it's made a huge difference for everyone. Someone reading this, maybe you, could be a harbinger of change and unlock a part of yourself and make something great happen.

In an upcoming chapter, I'll share the powerful science behind what I call a "Totem" or "Artifact," to "Activate" your Alter Ego.

After watching Joni's story, feeling inspired, I raced to the eyeglass store and bought a pair of prescription-free glasses, much to the bewilderment of the staff. "You're sure you want to buy glasses without a prescription?" the clerk asked.

"Yes, please."

"But you have perfect vision. Why would you want a pair of glasses?"

"Because I'm weird, okay? Can I just get the glasses, please?"

This was long before glasses became a fashion item like they are today.

I started wearing them when I dealt with prospective clients. Just like I used my persona on the sports field. I now transformed into Richard. (Richard is actually my first name, but I had always gone by Todd and still do today.) I put the glasses on *only* when I needed to be Richard, and I took them off as soon as business was over.

A PATTERN EMERGES

I spent years working with athletes before I realized that what I had used to give me an edge and to level up my performance was actually something other athletes used, too. I was speaking with one of my coaching clients, a swimmer with her eye on securing a spot on the Olympic swim team, when she mentioned how she became a different version of herself as soon as she dove into the pool.

There was something about her comment that made me pause and think, That's interesting. There was something about what she said that dislodged other, eerily similar comments that other athletes had said to me over the years. Until this point, I hadn't noticed or paid attention. I keep detailed notes on all my clients, so after she mentioned this "different version" of herself to me, I pawed through old notepads and computer files looking for other similar statements.

To my surprise, I didn't just find one or two athletes who said similar things. I found many.

They didn't call it an Alter Ego, a Secret Identity, or any other name. Some would call it "a different version of myself," like the Olympic-hopeful swimmer. Others said they would pretend to be someone from comics or movies, like Wolverine. A lot of athletes mentioned comic book or superhero characters, or sports heroes, as the person they imagined themselves to be.

Now that I had noticed the pattern, whenever a client mentioned they would step into a different version of themselves, I would ask what sort of prop they would use. I figured that since I used trading cards and eyeglasses, other people could use something similar to help this other version of themselves come out, too. My hunch was right. Many athletes had something they used.

It wasn't enough for me to notice the pattern. I wanted a way to use what I had found to help other athletes.

A NEW WAY

Athletes often struggle with feelings of judgment, worry, and criticism. Their inner critic is the reason many players don't take the last shot to tie the basketball game, why they strike out with runners on second and third with the score tied, or why they miss the putt to take the lead. Something gets in the way.

There are any one of a number of tools in the "inner game" tool kit we can use to help someone perform to their capabilities. Some of them are long-term strategies:

- Meditation
- Better instruction
- Relaxation and breathing control
- Imagery and visualization
- Skill development
- Routine development
- Goal-setting
- In some cases, even therapy

I used them while working with clients. However, when I was being called on a Thursday to help someone who had an important competition on a Saturday, I needed more than just long-term strategies. I needed to help someone *now*.

Some of the strategies already listed could be used in a tight time window, but I found that only one delivered consistent results, time after time. That is why it's been a pillar strategy, and why I happen to be known as the "Alter Ego guy" in pro sports.

Now that I'm two decades into my career, I have shared the strategy beyond the sports and entertainment world. I've seen people use the Alter Ego Effect to secure funding for their start-ups, become better parents, launch new online businesses, write books, and pursue goals they'd been sitting on for years.

I've talked about the Alter Ego Effect throughout the book so far. Now let me show you how it works and why it's so effective.

CHAPTER 3

THE POWER OF THE ALTER EGO EFFECT

Ian is a smart marketing professional and the founder of a multimillion-dollar e-commerce business. In his former life, Ian was a serious tennis player. "I wasn't just someone winning a few high school matches; in college I won a national championship," he told me.

A fierce competitor who since the age of three had a racket in hand, Ian had the physical abilities to go to the next level.

Sadly, those could only take him so far. "Ask anyone who played tennis with me and they'd tell you the same thing: I was a classic case of wasted potential. I had the physical capabilities, but I couldn't pull it together mentally or emotionally. I was a psychopath on the courts, breaking rackets and punching walls after I lost."

What drove Ian mad with anger, rage, and frustration? I mean, it was only a tennis match after all, right? Except, to Ian, it wasn't *just* a tennis match, and he wasn't *just* losing at some weekend match.

"In my mind, I wasn't losing a tennis match. I was failing as a human being because being a tennis player was my identity."

Okay, let's pause and replay that statement: *I was failing as a human being because being a tennis player was my identity.*

Does that resonate with you? If you're ambitious, it most likely does. Ian's prophetic statement lies at the beating heart of the Alter Ego Effect and the model I want to walk you through. The reasons why it's resonated with thousands of people and empowered people to make decisive changes are:

1. It makes sense and you already know how to do this.
2. It allows you to see the multidimensional person you are, with the different roles you play, and be intentional about who shows up where. So you don't bring a Clark Kent when who you need is a Superman.
3. It gets to the heart of why talented, capable people underperform. They don't realize it, but they're being unintentional about what "who" is showing up on their Field of Play and into those Moments of Impact.

What do I mean by "who is showing up"? Let me explain.

HOW DO YOU BECOME YOU?

Before I get into walking you through the stages of building your own Alter Ego or Secret Identity, I want to show you why it's so powerful and why it's very easy to slip into a version of yourself that isn't built to succeed. Over the next few pages, we're going to be building out a model to explain how we become what we become. Through the rest of the book, we'll use it to approach life with more confidence, courage, and conviction.

To start things off you need to understand you have a Core Self.

The Core Self is where possibility exists. It's this deep inner core where a creative force resides waiting to be activated by the power of intention. Because human beings have this incredible ability to imagine, create, and decide, it gives you the opportunity to change something in an instant. The Core Self is where your deep desires, aspirations, and dreams reside. If you've ever avoided admitting to yourself what you truly want, that's probably your Core Self talking to you. It's those internal nudges you get to take action and move toward something that excites you or "lights you up."

It's also the source of "intrinsic motivation." If you've ever found yourself trying to answer a question about "why you do something" or "why you care," but you can't find the words, you're probably being driven by an intrinsic motivator. They're the intangibles. Something you can't touch, hold, or show someone else. Human beings have a collection of intrinsic motivators that, when you tap into them, drive a more meaningful level of action.

Things like:

- Growth, the desire to improve and constantly get better
- Curiosity, the desire to discover new things
- Mastery, the desire to learn and become excellent at something
- Adventure, the desire to be challenged and explore the world and ourselves
- Enjoyment, the desire to feel satisfied with our efforts and lost in the moment
- Self-mastery, the desire to feel autonomous and to direct your own life
- Love, the desire to care deeply for someone or something

These intrinsic motivators are shared by everyone in some way or another. They're baked into the human condition. And they're extremely important to leading a life of meaning.

The problem arises when we start to confuse all the other layers that influence our thinking, emotions, and behaviors with who we really are. If you've ever tried to unravel the mystery of how you became who you are, it can feel like being caught in a spiderweb. The more you try, the more you wrap yourself up and get stuck. You can't explain why you became indecisive when faced with an important decision. You can't understand why you clam up and get nervous or second-guess ideas when you're in a room with certain people.

You don't know why you keep talking and talking during a sales call, which talks a potential customer out of the sale. Or why you keep dreaming about starting a business but it never happens.

It's critical to understand that at our core, we are a force for creative possibility, whatever that may be for you. You may have wondered how you became the way you are, or you said to yourself, ". . . but that's just me. That's just the way I am."

Maybe not.

Who we are, specifically the person we bring to our various Fields of Play and how we perform, is heavily influenced by external and internal factors.

I break these groups of influence into four layers that surround our Core Self. (If you'd like a complete map of the Field of Play Model, go to AlterEgoEffect.com/resources.)

LAYER 1: YOUR CORE DRIVERS (WHAT MOTIVATES YOU AT A GRANDER SCALE THAN YOURSELF)

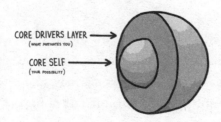

CORE DRIVERS LAYER ⟶ (WHAT MOTIVATES YOU)

CORE SELF ⟶ (YOUR POSSIBILITY)

This is where you'll find what you deeply care about, deeply relate to, and deeply identify with. These give you a sense of purpose and can often be things people feel define them. Your deeper purpose could be related to Family, Community, Nation, Religion, Race, Gender, Identifiable Group, Idea, or Cause. However, as you'll see, these Core Drivers, and any of the layers, can also affect you negatively as well.

LAYER 2: THE BELIEF LAYER (HOW YOU DEFINE YOURSELF AND THE WORLD AROUND YOU)

This is where you'll find your attitudes, beliefs, values, perceptions, experiences, and expectations toward how you see yourself and how you perceive the world around you. [Figure 3.2]

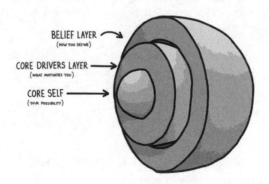

LAYER 3: THE ACTION LAYER (HOW YOU SHOW UP)

This represents the skills, competencies, and knowledge we've developed over time. It's also the behaviors, actions, and reactions we have on the Field of Play and during our Moments of Impact. [Figure 3.3]

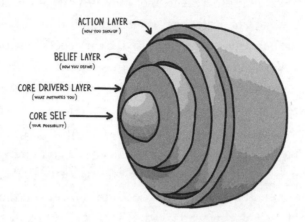

LAYER 4: THE FIELD OF PLAY (WHAT'S HAPPENING)

This is the area of context. In this layer, we're influenced by our actual physical environment; the circumstances; the constraints; the people, places, and things that we interact with; and their expectations. [Figure 3.4]

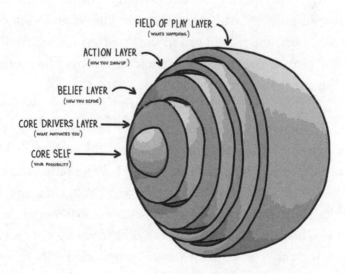

All of these layers influence and shape how you think, feel, and see yourself in relation to the different areas of your life or what we refer to as the Fields of Play. Each of those layers is built up over time. Often, we're unaware of some behavior, and it's because the influences are outside of our awareness. We're going to be looking at these layers more deeply and how to use them to change our results with the help of an Alter Ego.

You may see yourself as someone who's a kind and nice person. (Those are great qualities.) However, on the Field of Play of work, people may take advantage of that kindness and heap more work on you than is fair, or use it to negotiate unfair terms. Instead, I'm asking you to be more intentional about who needs to show up on that field. This isn't about dishonoring who you are. This is about really looking at the characteristics that will help you succeed, and bringing that part of you to life with the help of an Alter Ego.

FROM CHURCH CHOIR TO SOLD-OUT STADIUMS

Sundays were a day people looked forward to in the Black Bottom neighborhood on the East Side of Detroit. They'd wake up, put on their Sunday best, and head down to the St. John's United Methodist Church to "hear an angel sing." The choir was always filled with great singers, but there was one who stood out.

Jada came from a religious family that loved gospel music. Their home was filled with music, and she and her sister would belt out any tune you'd ask them to sing. The people in East Detroit loved it when she'd share her gift with them on Sunday. Her father recognized her unique voice and started taking Jada and her best friend, Alicia, around the Detroit area to talent competitions. After a while, their group of two became a group of six, and they formed a girl group that began rapping and dancing their way to competition wins.

As the years went by, this gospel-singing girl from a religious family started to gain more national attention, but a problem emerged. Jada found it hard to perform the more "suggestive" lyrics and dance moves onstage. But she loved the creative expression and freedom she felt up there. Her ambitions were creating an internal conflict.

Her solution? She turned to an Alter Ego, "Hailey Storm." Unlike, Jada, her "real self," Hailey embraced the provocateur. Hailey Storm wasn't afraid to shake, shimmy, and shine onstage in front of crowds that were swelling into the thousands. The young gospel-singing girl who grew up dazzling the parishioners of the church had grown into an international superstar.

Except, she wasn't actually from Detroit, her name isn't Jada, and her Alter Ego wasn't Hailey Storm. If you didn't already guess, this superstar is Beyoncé Knowles, from Houston, Texas, and her Alter Ego that helped bring her to fame was Sasha Fierce. However, St. John's United Methodist Church was the church she wowed people at every Sunday.

In multiple interviews, Beyoncé has mentioned how and why she used her Alter Ego:

"When I see a video of myself onstage or TV I'm like, 'Who is that girl?'"[1]

"I have created an alter ego: things I do when performing I would never do normally. I reveal things about myself that I wouldn't do in an interview."[2]

"I have out-of-body experiences [onstage]. If I cut my leg, if I fall I don't even feel it. I'm so fearless, I'm not aware of my face or my body."[3]

"I have someone else that takes over when it's time for me to work and when I'm onstage, this alter ego that I've created that kind of protects me and who I really am."[4]

Then famously, after her 2008 album, *I Am . . . Sasha Fierce*, she retired her Alter Ego. She didn't need her anymore. Whatever transformation or experimentation Beyoncé needed "Sasha" to help with as a performer was complete.

It may be difficult to look at your life and call yourself a "performer." You may not be "performing" in the context of a Beyoncé, Ellen DeGeneres, or David Bowie, with thousands of people expecting a "show," but if you think about "show" as simply a fulfillment of expectations, you'll see the parallels very quickly. We do have expectations to fulfill, "a show." We do have to perform our responsibilities, "a show." Many of us have ambitions buried inside us that are difficult and challenging, and demand something we're not quite sure we can fulfill, so why not use an Alter Ego?

You have stages you're already performing on and stages you might like to perform on, and my question is: Would you like to show up there as the heroic version of yourself?

I've spent more than fifteen thousand hours working one-on-one with elite performers like Olympians and CEOs, all the way down to ten-year-old kids. The Alter Ego Effect is and has been my weapon of choice when trying to help good people do hard things. It's also a very natural way humans can deal with adversity with more calm, cool, and confidence, and researchers at the University of Minnesota showed its effectiveness.

ACTIVATING YOUR HEROIC SELF

If you've already started to play with this concept in your head, maybe you've started to think, Hmm, it would be kind of cool to show up with a secret identity. If something doesn't work out, I don't need to be so hard on myself and my secret identity can take the blame. I can leave that identity on the field, like Beyoncé, and save my "Self" from the worries and judgments I normally kick myself with. (I'm taking a few liberties with your self-talk, but let's run with it, cool?)

Well, the idea of using Alter Egos to create some distance between how you currently see yourself and how you'd like to perform is not only smart, it's backed by research. A lot of my clients initially talk about how their Alter Egos protected them, only to later realize that their Alter Ego was actually who they always were and who they had always wanted to be.

This idea of space and distance between our identities is something that researchers are starting to validate. A recent University of Minnesota study of four- and six-year-old children found that to teach kids perseverance, parents should teach children to pretend to be like Batman or another favorite character—because it creates psychological distance,[5] the very thing my clients like Ian talk about, and what I've observed happens when people create Alter Egos.

The study split kids into three groups. The researchers put a toy in a locked glass box and gave the kids a ring of keys. The catch? No key worked. The researchers wanted to see how to improve the children's executive functioning skills and were interested in seeing how long they would try to unlock the box and what they would try. To help the kids, the researchers gave them what they called strategies. One strategy was to pretend to be Batman. The kids could even wear a cape! Dora the Explorer was a choice, too.[6]

Researchers found that the kids who worked the longest were the ones who impersonated Batman or Dora, followed by children who just pretended, and, finally, the kids who remained in the first-person perspective.[7] The kids impersonating Batman or Dora were more flexible thinkers, they tried the most keys, and they were calmer. One four-year-old even said, "Batman never gets frustrated."[8]

The study shows us the power of identity—the power of how we see ourselves—and what happens when we, for a moment in time, can call forth a different self.

Superman created Clark Kent so that society would accept him, so he could walk around unnoticed and never consider himself above everyone else. I created "Richard" so I could move away from my insecurities, launch my business, and better serve the people I wanted. Beyoncé created "Sasha Fierce" to explore her creative side and experiment with her art form.

I hope this starts to peel back the proverbial onion on why an Alter Ego becomes such an effective agent of change. When you become more intentional about what characteristics will show up on an important Field of Play for you, you'll Activate a creative energy powering a new level of performance.

If Ian had recognized that just *one* Field of Play doesn't define him as a person, he could have avoided the emotional outbursts, frustration, and mental grenades going off in his head.

THE ORDINARY AND EXTRAORDINARY WORLD

I'm going to reinforce this point throughout the book because I don't want you to get a sugary sweet taste in your mouth from the words on the page. You're not a terrible human being if some area of your life is "average." You won't put this book down and become Batman, Black Widow, or Black Panther in EVERY. SINGLE. AREA. OF. YOUR. LIFE.

Frankly, I'd kick my own ass if that was the book I wrote.

Instead, treat this idea like a compass, orientating you to *one* stage. Find one Field of Play, and let's look at creating something extraordinary there. It'll make this process far simpler, far more accessible, and a helluva lot easier to implement.

In this section, I want to simply give you the landscape of what's happening in what is called the "Ordinary World" and the "Extraordinary World" inside the Field of Play Model and prepare you for the journey ahead. [Figure 3.5]

FIELD OF PLAY MODEL

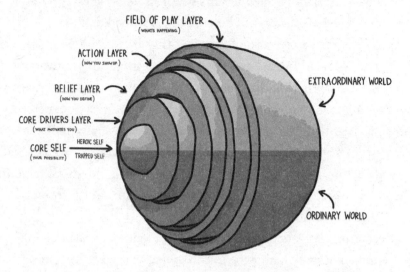

The terms *ordinary* and *extraordinary* are in essence metaphors we use to orient you to the common experience you'll have when you shift your mindset. Also, the short- and long-term effects of your "orientation" will affect your level of confidence to face the challenges ahead. There's also research to support the positive effects of this shift in mindset.

Researchers have found that "self-suppressive activation" and "self-expansive activation" are keys to opening the vault to more confidence and courage.[9] [10] In the research and work we've done, we refer to it as the Ow Mindset and the Wow Mindset. Suppressing the Ow Mindset means your intentions and actions are motivated by negative emotions; you're trying to prevent bad things from happening. Whether they're thoughts, feelings, or experiences, you're "suppressing" to avoid perceived pain, the Ow Mindset.

If you approach any activity to avoid a challenge, it's a form of suppression. When you set the orientation, like a compass, to negative motivation and do something to avoid some pain, or avoid something altogether, it makes it more difficult to see yourself as the person who can solve your own problems. This suppressive cycle of avoiding who you are and who you want to be creates a Trapped Self.

"Self-expansive activation," on the other hand, and what we refer to as the "Wow Mindset," is when your intentions are motivated by a positive or growth mindset. You're trying to activate or gain something more in life, whether it's positive thoughts, emotions, or experiences. Setting the orientation to positive emotion and being motivated to create something positive in your life, over the long term, habitually and as a routine, enhances your self-efficacy. It builds your confidence, courage, and sense of control over your ability to face life's challenges; it creates a Heroic Self.

Becoming clear about your intentions, identifying the benefits you get from an activity, and determining what you want to achieve on a Field of Play is what will help unlock your Heroic Self.

Easier said than done, right?

That's why we use Alter Egos and Secret Identities; they help us suspend any disbelief and leverage the power of aligning with someone or something else's strengths, capabilities, and superpowers.

So, to help you see how this plays out in the Alter Ego Effect, there are two worlds we've created. We live in a world of opposites, up/down, hot/cold, outside/inside, light/dark, and on and on. The separation is there to delineate the worlds we can choose to live in, the Ordinary and the Extraordinary World. Each of these creates two totally different experiences. Neither is devoid of challenge, but both create a useful view of what happens when we choose to "suppress" or "expand" our Core Self.

We're going to be expanding on these more in the coming chapters as we build out your Alter Ego, but you can see that the separation of these two worlds has created another zone at the center of the Core Self.

In the Ordinary World you can find a Trapped Self, and in the

Extraordinary World you can find a Heroic Self. Both of these represent the typical experience someone feels, depending on how they're approaching and experiencing a Field of Play.

This is why we call it the Alter Ego Effect. It creates a completely new result or outcome.

If you imagine standing at the center of the Field of Play Model, and you turn to face the Ordinary World, the common thoughts, emotions, and experiences you have as you move through each of those layers "suppress" your Core Self and you end up feeling Trapped.

How?

As with any good story, if there is a hero, there is also an *Enemy* lurking in the shadows. And because your orientation has been set to "negative or pain," the Enemy feeds off it and fills you with doubt, worry, self-judgment, avoidance, and fear. All of this can cause you to not show up on a particular Field of Play like you're capable of and in some cases, not show up at all. Basically, you completely avoid the field or you avoid letting all of your abilities shine. The reason is that you've been hit with the powerful Hidden Forces the Enemy deploys to keep you trapped.

The Enemy uses all the layers to challenge you. It tells you things like:

- The Core Drivers Layer:
  - "You're not meant for that; after all, nobody from your family has ever done that before."
- The Belief Layer:
  - "You don't believe in yourself, because if you just take a look at your past, you've quit on a lot of things."
- The Action Layer:
  - "You don't have the skills or knowledge, so you should probably just wait until you do more research, work on it more, and finally get it perfect."

- The Field of Play Layer:
  - "You don't want to make a fool of yourself. Are you sure you want to take such a huge risk? I'd hate for everyone to see what happens if you fail!"

The common experience in the Ordinary World is this sense that it's not you running the show. It's this feeling like the "real you" is trapped by some negative story, belief, or circumstance you can't find a way to overcome. But the Enemy is a wily little bugger and it's always waiting any time it senses just a bit of trepidation, negative motivation, and lack of clear intent on who is going to show up on a Field of Play.

The Ordinary World can be summed up with two words: *destructive* and *uninspired*. It is destructive to our Core Self and uninspired through our results. So it's important to realize that this Trapped Self, which most people feel is who they are, isn't you. The Core Self has resources available to activate a different side of you, the Heroic Self, with the help of an Alter Ego.

So, is everything in the Extraordinary World all sunshine and rainbows?

If you go back to the center of the Field of Play Model, and you turn to face the Extraordinary World, the common thoughts, emotions, and experiences you have as you move through each of those layers "expand" your Core Self and you end up feeling Heroic.

How?

In the Extraordinary World, your "orientation" has been set to "positive." The Enemy has a harder time stopping you with its arrows of doubt, temptation, anger, ego, and fear because you build an Alter Ego using all of the layers to bring a powerful set of characteristics or *Superpowers* onto a specific Field of Play. You activate this creative force from your Core Self to show up like you want to. And you say things like:

- The Core Drivers Layer:
  - "I'm doing this for my family." "I'm doing this for a greater cause." "I'm doing this to show others in my tribe what can be done." "I'm doing this to honor the people who came before me."
- The Belief Layer:
  - "I am a powerful force for change." "I love the challenge." "I can't wait to see what happens."
- The Action Layer:
  - "I may not know everything, but I'll give it my best." "I have this incredible power to focus on what's important." "I'm extremely calm in high-pressure situations."
- The Field of Play Layer:
  - "Failure is a block I turn into a stepping-stone." "I've got so many allies, waiting to help me."

The Extraordinary World is extraordinary because we tackle life head-on, we challenge it, and we don't let distractions slow us down. It also allows you to suspend disbelief about your capabilities, because you're taking an Alter Ego onto the Field of Play. And this Alter Ego, just like Beyoncé's, Sasha Fierce, protects your Core Self from the tools the Enemy uses to stop you. Plus, it turns out there's research to back up the power of intentionally bringing predefined Superpowers to your world.

Martin Seligman and Christopher Petersen are two of the most widely cited researchers of happiness and well-being.[11] Over the period of a decade, they studied almost one hundred cultures around the globe. The team tested 150,000 people to determine how people that were coping with adversity and the challenges of life operated. They found that the people who identified their core characteristics or Superpowers and deliberately and intentionally focused on Activating those Superpowers were more resilient and fulfilled.

We'll be digging into uncovering those Superpowers your Alter Ego will Activate throughout the book.

THE IMAGINATION GAME

You and I have this incredibly powerful ability to create worlds in the mind with our imaginations. Most people are unfortunately using their imaginations to play out scenarios that look like horror stories. It causes them to retract and move away from their goals. But if I asked them to imagine themselves showing up in that same scenario as Wonder Woman, Mother Teresa, or Princess Leia, they could imagine a very different result. (For the guys, you can imagine yourself as Superman, Nelson Mandela, or Yoda. But if you want to be Wonder Woman, I won't judge.)

Let's play a quick imagination game.

Scenario:

You have to give a speech to a thousand of your peers in a huge auditorium.

How would *you* perform?

Would you be nervous? What would your body language look like? How would you sound to others?

Now imagine yourself going onstage as Wonder Woman or Superman. How would you act, look, and sound now?

What about as Mother Teresa or Nelson Mandela?

Or Princess Leia or Yoda?

Now, here's one of the most important points of the book, so pay close attention.

From an observer's perspective, who is the "real you"?

Be careful how you answer, because this is the paradox that has tripped up most people in their lives. It is also how many people in the amateur self-help world have led people astray for decades.

To help you with your answer, think of it this way:

We are judged in our lives by what we do, *not* by what we think or intend to do.

If I think about calling my mom and telling her exactly why I love her, and I *actually* pick up the phone and call and tell her, it creates a totally different world. One is Ordinary, the other Extraordinary.

If you show up for a speech incredibly nervous but everyone in the audience *experiences* you as being confident, articulate, and funny, does it really matter to them if you showed up as an "Alter Ego" in order to give them that experience and yourself the reward?

No.

At the end of the day, I care about how people perform.

When I first started my business, I wanted to be a confident, decisive, and articulate professional who could help athletes get better results on their Fields of Play by improving their mental toughness. The problem? That person wasn't showing up. I was trapped by one of the Hidden Forces the Enemy likes to use to snuff out action taking: worrying about what other people would think of me. People weren't going to respect me or listen to me because I looked so young. Those doubts, worries, and fears rattling around inside my head got in the way. But when I slipped on a pair of glasses, my Alter Ego stepped forth, activating the specific traits, skills, and beliefs I wanted so I could perform. They were there all along, and "Richard" stepped in to make them happen.

This isn't being fake. Pretending to know about particle physics when you don't is fake. Using an Alter Ego to entertain a group of physics students when you have been a boring physics professor until now is just bringing the right tools for the job.

One of my favorite parts about the feedback I get from clients and people is the sense of amazement people have about the depth and breadth of their abilities. This is the classic case of "it's hard to read the label when you're inside the bottle."

Michael Shurtleff, a Broadway and Hollywood casting director in the 1960s and 1970s, said that acting, contrary to what many people believed, is about tapping into what already exists inside. "Most people go into acting to get out of themselves, to get away from their everyday humdrum selves, and become someone else who is glamorous, romantic, unusual, different. And what does acting turn out to be? Using your own self. Working from what's inside you. Not being someone else but being you in different situations and contexts. Not escaping you but using yourself naked and exposed up there on the stage or silver screen."[12]

Daniel Craig isn't James Bond. But James Bond is somewhere inside Daniel Craig.

Most of my clients say the Alter Ego feels more like their truest self—I'll let you judge that for yourself later. My good friend Ian says, "The Alter Ego is your deepest self, the truest version of you."

This was Joanne's experience, too. Joanne, who was trained in cognitive behavioral therapy and transactional analysis, began her career working for yacht brokers before working in sales and marketing on the technology side for British Airways in London. A self-described introvert by nature, she had a side that would come out at the office that she never quite understood.

"I had experiences early in my career, like getting blocked for a promotion after I landed a huge global deal and after handling accounts worth millions of dollars, that made me realize I had to take charge of my career. I had to go out there and get my career myself. I wasn't going to leave it in anyone else's destiny."

Joanne knew she needed to show up differently in her job if she was to succeed. Working in a largely male-dominated world, Joanne began to switch into a strong, bold, decisive woman in meetings with her peers and boss.

When Joanne first heard me talk about the Alter Ego, it was like everything clicked for her. "When I heard you talk about it, I thought,

That's Giovanna! I'm part Italian, and when I go into certain work settings, I switch from being the quiet girl who sits in the background into this other persona that has no hang-ups. Where I may normally worry about what someone thinks of me, Giovanna doesn't think any of that.

"All along, Giovanna has shielded and protected me, and helped me to go places I've always dreamed of."

When we talked about the concept of protection, she explained that when she was in a toxic environment, where people "did and said unsavory things," having her Alter Ego helped her realize "it was other people and their issues, not me. I could walk away from the circumstances and the people. You'd walk away from something someone said or did in the boardroom, thinking, This is terrible, but Giovanna could take it. As Giovanna, I stood up for myself. As Giovanna, I can come across as fierce and powerful and scary when I needed to."

Joanne's Alter Ego was helping her stay rooted in her true sense of Core Self, without succumbing to the poisonous whispers of the Enemy.

"I used to worry that I was too harsh with someone, but I wouldn't be where I am if I didn't allow my Alter Ego to take charge and be fierce. There's no place in business if you're not able to step up for yourself and be fierce when you need to be." Using her Alter Ego of Giovanna helped Joanne to show up as the best version of herself so she could accomplish her work goals.

"Over the last two years, I've realized that the Alter Ego is actually who I am, and ultimately, who I'd love to continue being."

Like Ian, Beyoncé, and Joanne, your Alter Ego is really about defining how you want to show up, defining the Superpowers, and borrowing the characteristics of an existing person, character, superhero, animal, or whatever to help Activate your Heroic Self.

You get to define who shows up on the Field of Play. The layers that make up your experience of life are fluid, and as I walk you through building your Alter Ego, you'll get to create the outcome. Which will end up being the most real, most true version of your Core Self?

Over the years, psychologists have noticed the benefits of using the Alter Ego concept, too. Psychologist Oliver James chronicles how the late entertainer David Bowie created a number of Alter Egos, including Ziggy Stardust, to achieve his ambition of rock stardom and to overcome an abusive, damaging childhood. James even makes the case that Bowie achieved success and became an emotionally healthy man *because* he created these personas. "The key was the therapeutic use he had made of personas to develop authentic selves."[13] (Even David Bowie was actually a persona, as the famous entertainer was born David Jones.)

The idea of different personas wasn't confined to only a select few or only to elite performers like Bowie. As James explains, "Working as a therapist, I have not met a single client who does not have several or numerous different selves."[14] James even advocates that all of us can use different personas to achieve our goals, too, just like David Jones used David Bowie and Ziggy Stardust to achieve his, "understanding the different parts of yourself better, identifying them and their origins, and then being much more self-conscious about which person you choose to be in different settings."[15]

That's all we're doing with the Alter Ego—we're consciously and intentionally choosing to bring the best version of our "selves" forward for the different roles we play in life.

YOU MAY ALREADY BE DOING THIS

I've coached, taught, and presented on the Alter Ego Effect for almost two decades. After I explain the concept to people, just about everyone tells me they've used an Alter Ego or aspects of one without realizing it.

That's what happened to Kisma, the founder of a coaching and training company. When she first learned about the Alter Ego Effect, she realized that she'd used a variation of it in her previous life as a professional musician.

"Playing in professional orchestras, there is a certain level of nerves I would feel before solos. I played the flute and performed a number of concertos, and I had to get into a different mindset. As I would walk across the stage, preparing myself for the concerto, I would think, Who do I want to channel? Who do I want to be like? Sometimes it was Yo-Yo Ma, other times it was Emmanuel Pahud. Whoever I chose, it was like an instant drop-in, as I told myself that I would pull from them."

Without knowing it, Kisma was leveraging some elements of the Alter Ego Effect to show up on her Field of Play and appear during her Moments of Impact—her solos. But she didn't realize she could use it in other aspects of her life, especially her business, until we met.

A lot of people are like Kisma—maybe even you. They've intuitively tapped into their imagination and created an Alter Ego. They just haven't used it to its fullest extent and intentionally, but they recognize its form. It's familiar to them. They just didn't have a name for it or a process.

Now it's time to choose your adventure, because just as there are many ways to get to the center of town, the Alter Ego Effect has many doorways you can enter and walk through . . .

CHAPTER 4

YOUR ORDINARY WORLD

"There's no way to describe it other than, I felt trapped. Every morning I had the intention of sitting down at my kitchen table to write, but it was like the chair and my butt were magnets that repelled each other. The resistance was incredible, and I felt like I was trapped in this purgatory of wanting to create something, but not having the power to overcome the resistance."

I sat in my airplane seat listening to a well-known author recount what it was like to struggle to pursue his lifelong dream. The funny thing about being in my line of work is that it opens people up to sharing their challenges in life. It always makes for great conversations, especially with people who found a way to overcome those challenges.

He went on to tell me that even when he did sit down to write, he'd stare at the blinking cursor on his computer screen and with every flash of the cursor imagine it was saying, "You can't do this. You can't do this. You can't do this."

"It haunted me every time."

He also had a small globe sitting on a shelf nearby that he'd stare at blankly. He said, "I'd stare at that thing for an eternity and get lost in this endless spiral of self-talk that I wasn't 'cut out to write' or whatever words I typed out were going to be rubbish anyway. It was crushing to my soul."

Before I finished the thirty-thousand-foot conversation with the accomplished author, here's what I knew: He wasn't a special snow-flake. His experience wasn't particularly unique.

I've spoken to car enthusiasts who wanted to rebuild and restore a car from scratch, spent years collecting magazines and ordering boxes of parts, and even planned a Saturday to start their project only to walk into their garage, sit on a stool, and watch those boxes collect dust.

I've heard stories from sales reps who started out driving their cars into vacant parking lots, reclining their seats to hide, and sitting there for hours because they were terrified of knocking on doors to sell their widget.

One man even said, "When I put my finger on the electric recline button on my seat and flicked it back, it was like I was sinking into the quicksand of fear. And this heavy weight would start to build on my chest and get heavier and heavier the more I reclined. It was terrible."

I've heard athletes tell me about the games they'd play and never attempt a shot because "that was for [insert any name of a better player] to do, not me."

I could go on and on with stories from artists, singers, actors, scientists, students, corporate professionals, traders, mothers, and entrepreneurs, of how some force was stopping them from moving toward their goals or dreams.

This is what is known as the *Ordinary World*.

It's a world where it feels like the "real you" is trapped. The you that has aspirations, dreams, and goals that aren't being actualized. They aren't getting out onto the Field of Play so you can see just how good you are or what you can do. It's frustrating, stressful, and typically creates a pile of self-judgment.

It's also a very easy place to stay stuck, because it's not life-or-death for most people. I mean, it's not like there's a saber-toothed tiger chasing you down and going to devour you. *Unless* you take action, right? It's an internal world *you* know about, filled with aspirations, hopes, dreams, goals, and visions of a better, different, or more evolved version of who you are today.

It's not like you're a character on a movie screen and the whole audience knows these struggles exist.

It's an easy place to stay trapped. There's an internal justification of "Nobody will ever know anyway if I don't do this."

But you will always know.

YOUR ORDINARY WORLD

By now, you might already be thinking about what your Alter Ego will be, or your Superpower, or maybe just what problem you need solved. There's no one way to get started. Choose what's best for you. Start where you're comfortable. If you get stuck somewhere, skip to the next step. It's that simple.

For the book, I've laid out the chapters to begin by delving into the Ordinary World first. Then I'll help you see the Common and Hidden Forces the Enemy likes to use to suppress and keep you trapped. I'll help you reveal what has influenced you in the past and what part of yourself has been showing up on your Field of Play and during your Moment of Impact.

As you move through this chapter you'll decide which Field of Play you'll focus on, so you can enter the lab and create your first Alter Ego. Let's examine this idea of a Field of Play and uncover what's "ordinary" about it. Or possibly reveal those Moments of Impact on your field when you feel discouraged, frustrated, and disappointed because you're not showing up like you want or can and maybe get trapped by any of the Hidden Forces.

Now, we're not going to lay you down on a psychologist's sofa and unravel years and years of trauma, because, frankly, it's not needed.

The power of the Alter Ego Effect is rooted in its simplicity, and how fast you can apply it to get results.

When I first start working with my clients or people I meet and ask them what problems/challenges/frustrations they're facing, they'll tell me things like:

SPORTS

"I'm not taking enough shots during the game."

"My coach is harder on me than my teammates."

"I'm in a slump and I don't know how to get out of it."

"I have a big tryout coming up and I need to perform at my best."

"I'm overthinking things too much on the field."

BUSINESS

"I'm launching a new business but I'm struggling to get new customers."

"I can't find investors for my start-up."

"I'm not sure what I should do next to grow the company."

"My staff is killing me."

"I'm fed up that my business isn't growing and I'm burnt out."

CAREER

"It's freaking painful that I can't finish my manuscript."

"I'm a nice person, and I like being a nice person, but in business, people are walking all over me."

"I'm tired of working so many hours and not getting recognized for my work."

"My entire industry is shifting and the uncertainty is stressing me out."

"I hate walking the red carpet and doing the media tours. All I want to do is act."

I could go on and on in the areas of finance, health and fitness, family, relationships, and personal time and well-being, but I'm sure you get the picture. Life is a challenge.

Ask yourself:

What is it about a particular area of your life that's frustrating you? What's making it "Ordinary"?

What don't you like about it?

What's not working in it?

What do you feel you're capable of doing that you're not?

You know yourself better than anyone. And your ability to be honest and real with yourself here is going to set you up for a lot more success later on in this book. There's no need to beat yourself up, shame yourself, or judge harshly. Allow yourself to be objective and real.

YOUR FIELD OF PLAY

"John is a beast, man! He's relentless and one of the most inspiring people I've ever met."

This was the most common remark I heard from the employees of a client when I interviewed them about their boss back in 2011. John was a proud "Italian Bronx kid" who loved his mom's manicotti and said "bro" more than anyone I'd ever met.

John had flown me into Houston to meet with his staff to help improve the performance and morale of his trading and brokerage company. Ever since the 2008 and 2009 financial meltdown, the company had taken a beating and he was struggling to keep the business profitable. He wanted my help to get his team "running on all cylinders" and "clear up some head trash" that had started to create a toxic environment.

Over the course of a few days, I met with thirty-five different team members, from Sylvia the diligent executive assistant to Marcus the stressed-out broker. And each of them would follow John into battle.

After talking to all the team members over a few days, John and I sat in his meticulously decorated office with sports memorabilia lining the walls and filling the shelves of his bookcases. We unpacked the events of the past few days and talked about the future.

When John originally reached out to me, he had heard about me from an NBA client who was his friend. I'd helped the friend build out an Alter Ego and John was interested in doing so, too, because he felt like he lost his edge.

Now sitting there, months after we started working together, I asked him, "How's your Alter Ego working out for you?"

"You should probably ask my wife and kids that question!" he said and laughed.

"So it's working."

"Bro! You have no idea. You nailed it. She's got a stack of cannolis waiting for you to take back to Nu Yahk."

Earlier, I mentioned how we have different roles we play in life. Each of these roles—parent, spouse, business owner, leader, sister, son—corresponds to a Field of Play. You can pick any Field of Play that you want to build an Alter Ego for and, just like John, you might automatically default to thinking about your professional life, sport, or vocation.

But in John's case, he discovered he didn't need any more help with his business. He already had a great work ethic and good attitude, and his current working persona was already a "beast." His home life, though, was a completely different story.

He'd grown up in a family where his dad was never around, and when he was around he was either yelling at the kids or buried in "his chair" ignoring everyone. John's home life was starting to mirror his father's and he hated it. So instead of taking more of his energy and devoting it to his work, we diverted it to his home-life Field of Play.

John built out his Alter Ego to be like his best friend's dad back in New York growing up. "Timmy's dad was always roughhousin' with us, crackin' jokes, threw the best neighborhood barbecues, and just flat-out loved life. He was fun to be around."

John found out through the process that the more he turned his attention to creating an inspiring home life, the more it transformed his work life, and his team loved him for it.

I mentioned that his team called him a "beast" over and over again. Now here's the thing: they already had respect for his work ethic and business savvy, but they called him a "beast" and "inspiring" because of what he had become at home.

As you work through this book, I'd encourage you to think about one Field of Play to build your Alter Ego for.

Is it your personal life? Some people lead phenomenal professional lives, easily achieving success. But when you look at their personal lives, they are less than ideal. They have no idea how to connect or form intimate, loving, stable relationships with their significant others, family, friends, or kids. Although most of my work with clients starts in their professional worlds or athletic worlds, as with John we often slip into their personal lives when they realize they want to be a better spouse or a parent.

Do you want an Alter Ego for your professional life? Some people lead awesome personal lives. They have loving, supportive relationships, but when it comes to achieving success professionally, they haven't made the impact they dream of.

I recommend going with the Field of Play that's causing you the most frustration, angst, or heartache. It's the one where building an Alter Ego is going to make a monumental impact on your life.

By the way, there are two reasons I call it the Field of Play. The first one is the obvious reference to the sports world and the idea that there are chalk lines, borders, and a starting and end point to the activity happening on the field. This is to help you recognize that we carry ourselves into many different fields in our lives, many different stages and arenas. And each one demands a different set of skills, attitudes, and mindsets to be successful.

It's one of the reasons why the Alter Ego Effect is so powerful: you become truly intentional about who's ending up on that field.

The second reason I use Field of Play is because of the final word, *play*. It's to remind you that you can have fun with this process. Life is already hard enough, and serious things or real struggles are a natural part of the unfolding of life. But that doesn't mean you can't take that same playful attitude you had when you were a kid and play with this concept and have fun with it.

It's exactly what John did, and now it's your turn.

THE LITTLE SHOP OWNER THAT COULD

MaryAnn and her husband opened an automotive repair shop in 1999. Her biggest challenge was her customers. She had come from the banking world, so she understood the financial pillar of running a business. But when customers called and she was the one to answer, they didn't want to talk with her. They wanted to speak to a technician or owner—they wanted to speak to a man, not a woman.

"I was frustrated with people," MaryAnn admits. "But when I stayed up one night and thought about it, and asked, 'What am I really frustrated with?' I realized it was myself, and my inability to walk people through that process and help them."

MaryAnn knew she was smart and competent, but she didn't sound like it on the phone, so of course people didn't want to speak to her. She set out to do two things. First, she had to go get the skills and knowledge she needed, then second, she created an Alter Ego to help her show up the way she wanted during her Moment of Impact (the customer phone call).

Before long, people were calling to specifically talk to her about their vehicle issues, and she especially made other women comfortable because they were being helped by a woman in an industry dominated by men.

What's happening in your Ordinary World may also be what's *not* happening. It could be what you're avoiding. Maybe you started a business, but you aren't out there getting the message out about your new products or services or making sales calls. Maybe you want to start a business, but you haven't. Maybe you want to ask for a raise or a promotion, but you haven't.

It's the classic and often-quoted quip from hockey legend Wayne Gretzky, "You miss one hundred percent of the shots you don't take."

Maybe you have what I call "focus-itis," the inability to focus on one thing and get it finished, which leaves you with a lot of wasted effort and nothing to show for the blood, sweat, and tears.

Whatever it might be, use this framework to get clear about your Ordinary World, so we can unleash your true performance capabilities.

THE FIVE BRIDGES TO PROGRESS

Quick question: Have you paid attention to the content or topic of the conversations you've had with people lately?

I can guarantee they'll fall into one of the following Five Bridges. I refer to them as bridges because bridges are pathways to allow things to come in and out of an area. For you, these Five Bridges can either help or hurt the quality of your professional, athletic, or personal life.

- Stopping
- Starting
- Continuing
- Less of
- More of

The vast majority of life's conversations when it comes to someone changing something is found in one of those five intentions.

"I want to stop smoking . . . stop eating unhealthy . . . stop drinking so much . . . stop going to bed so late . . . stop yelling at my kids . . . stop leaving things to the last minute . . ."

"I want to start eating more vegetables . . . start working out in the morning . . . start marketing my business more consistently . . . start having more fun . . . start spending evenings with my kids . . ."

"I want to continue working out . . . I want to continue my pregame routine . . . I want to continue engaging on social media for my business . . . I want to continue having weekly team meetings . . ."

"I want to watch less TV . . . I want to spend less time on social media . . . I want to feel less tired after lunch . . . I want to spend less time with that toxic group of people . . ."

"I want to read more good books . . . I want to go on more date nights with my wife . . . I want to hang out with friends more . . . I want to swim more . . . I want to laugh more . . ."

If you really started to pay attention to your life, you'd find these topics repeat themselves hourly. For the purposes of this exercise and to help you uncover even more helpful material to work with on our quest, we're going to add one final filter to your Five Bridges.

Thinking, feeling, doing, and experiencing.

These are the four planes we're always living in: What are you thinking, what are you feeling, what are you doing, and what are you experiencing or getting as a result?

In the context of your Ordinary World and the Field of Play you've chosen, we're going to use the Five Bridges framework throughout the book to help you get clear about what's working and not working and power up your Alter Ego. Because we're specifically talking about the results or outcomes you'd like to change, we'll only be using two of the "bridges" to help define your Ordinary World on the specific

Field of Play you've chosen. Make a list for each category below, and ask yourself, "What do I want to . . ."

- Stop experiencing/stop getting as a result or outcome
- Experience less of/get less of

To make it easier for you, these results would all be things you could hear, see, taste, touch, or smell. For example, maybe you want to:

- Stop not seeing my creative work get out there
- Experience less incomplete work
- Stop seeing my sales numbers decline
- Hear fewer people complain about my cooking/painting/writing or creative work
- Stop seeing my day wasted with social media
- Stop living where I'm at
- Lose less
- Stop hearing my coach criticize my poor performance
- Spend less
- Eat less
- Hear less rejection
- Make fewer bogies as a golfer
- Take fewer penalties
- Spend less time on the bench
- Spend less time at home
- Stop seeing my to-do list grow
- Stop hearing my family criticize me or tell me to get motivated

(To get more inspiration from others, go to AlterEgoEffect.com /tribe.)

When I'm working with a client, I have them do a huge data dump. Be free and honest while making this list. Don't try to censor or edit right now. The beauty of this exercise is that it gets you superclear on your Ordinary World, the results, and the outcomes that you're currently experiencing. Once you have this list made, then you can star the biggest priorities.

You may not be able to do everything. If you want an effective Alter Ego, you need to focus on one Field of Play. Get disciplined and focus on building a powerful Alter Ego that will change how you show up on your Field of Play.

The great thing about the Five Bridges of Progress exercise is that it really allows you to reflect on the entirety of your Field of Play. It forces you to get real about how you're currently living, acting, feeling, and thinking in your Ordinary World. But then it flips immediately into something positive. Instead of dwelling on what you want to stop or what isn't working, we're going to flip to what you do want and what you want to start experiencing—this is the Extraordinary World. But we'll get to that in a few chapters.

I often tell my clients, "I don't care what your answers are," and I don't. Each of us chooses to live our lives. All I concern myself with is whether my clients' actions, thoughts, and emotions are aligned with what they really want. When we're aligned, that's when the magic happens. Most of us aren't aligned. We're fighting against an internal tension that has a deep desire to be living in an Extraordinary World, if there was only something "outside of us" that would change. Don't stay trapped by this thinking, because that's where the Enemy lives.

Just be honest with yourself. Being honest with yourself is how you'll find the emotional resonance—the driving force, the purpose—that will fuel the Alter Ego.

FINISHING THE CONVERSATION AT
THIRTY THOUSAND FEET

As the famous author told me more about his backstory, I wrestled with a thought: Why was he so passionate about that globe? Well, I was about to get my answer.

"So how did you finally make the switch and defeat the resistance?" I asked.

He laughed and said, "Procrastination, oddly enough."

"Oh, really?"

"Yes. I was sitting in my armchair reading a book about the famous French novelist Victor Hugo, and something in his story struck me. It was the quote, 'Nothing is more powerful than an idea whose time has come.' It hit me like a book upside the head. I felt like he was speaking to me.

"So I got up from the chair, walked over to my shelf, grabbed the small globe, placed it on my desk, and rotated the country of France to face me, and I began to channel Victor Hugo. Victor became my writing Alter Ego. The words started to flow out of me, because 'my time had come.'"

So, do you have a clear picture in your head of your Ordinary World?

Do you know what's frustrating you?

If you do, great, because *your* time has come to step into your Extraordinary World.

CHAPTER 5

FINDING YOUR
MOMENTS OF IMPACT

We sat inside a boardroom, with a wall of glass surrounding us, over-looking the concrete jungle of New York City, watching thousands of New Yorkers racing around far below.

Shaun and I were looking out at the landscape while he was pointing out the buildings across the city where he had clients. It was an impressive collection of tall skyscrapers. Shaun is the head of cloud storage at a large technology company and works exclusively with the world's biggest banks and financial institutions. Shaun and I met because I was mentoring his daughter, an elite soccer player. After he saw what we were implementing to help her perform more consistently, he wanted the same high-performance strategies for his own career.

We walked back over to the big table and he sat down. I picked up a set of red, blue, and black markers and turned to the whiteboard to get to work. Today was the day we were going to map out a plan for his goal of being the number one sales producer in the company. No small feat, because he was working at a Fortune 50 organization.

I asked him what a normal day looked like. He told me about client meetings, giving presentations, dinners, talking to people on the phone, and handling some administrative work.

"What are you paid to do? Like what is your boss judging you on in your performance reviews?" I wanted him to drill down and get hyperspecific on his performance. I wanted him to get crystal clear about what would truly move the needle on his career.

"I'm hired to grow the cloud computing market in New York City, specifically the financial market."

"Great. And how are you doing in the eyes of your bosses?" I asked.

"Good. I hit my numbers."

"Is 'hitting your numbers' what you want?"

"No. I know I can be doing a lot more and I'm leaving a lot in the tank."

"Okay, well, let's look at your Field of Play and work backward from the ultimate goal of closing more deals and see if we can identify the things we need to change to make it happen."

TARGET MAPPING

Target mapping is defining your final outcome or goal and then working backward from that target to build a strategy and plan to reach the goal. Others call it "end-in-mind." Extremely successful people in any walk of life have a fantastic ability to think this way. If you ever find yourself feeling like you're walking a bit aimlessly, it's most likely because you haven't defined a destination, goal, or outcome and you're just "doing."

Picking a target and then working backward helps you see all the important steps or stages you need to reach in order for that desired end result to happen.

Want to wake up refreshed and rested at six every morning?

Want to have $1 million in investments working for you in ten years?

Want to end a tournament with your hands raised, feeling victorious and ecstatic about your performance?

Want to have a lean, fit, and healthy body you're proud of in ninety days?

Want to show up at the airport ninety minutes before your flight?

Then work backward to map out a plan with the steps that will ensure it happens. Does it mean you'll reach your goal with 100 percent certainty? Of course not. However, you've just increased the likelihood by a vast margin.

Once I could help Shaun get clear about his real purpose in the company—growing the cloud computing revenues in the financial market in New York City to a specific level—it would be easier to eliminate the distractions and focus his energy on the actions that matter.

Working backward, we keyed in on the actions that would have a real impact on whether he grew the financial market in New York. The list we made included things like client meetings, calls reaching out to prospective clients, relationship-building lunches, and presentations. These were the important activities on Shaun's career Field of Play. If we were talking about his family, personal well-being, or sports Fields of Play, the activities would look different, obviously. But Shaun was focused on creating excellence in this part of his career, so that's where we focused.

We broke down these activities and looked closely at his performance on the Field of Play. These are what I refer to as Moments of Impact. They're the actions, opportunities, events, situations, or expectations with the greatest impact on your success. Moments of Impact are filled with the most resistance, most emotion, and most challenge because they occur when you might be the most vulnerable.

It could be:

Asking for the sale
Taking the shot
Putting your words on paper and writing

Making a speech in front of a crowd

Speaking up when you hear something wrong

Apologizing

Saying, "I love you"

Investing your money

Submitting your resume

Taking a test

This is the place on the Field of Play Model where the Action Layer meets the Field of Play Layer. [Figure 3.5] These are those moments where you may be judged by others for your actions, your results, and your response. The Common and Hidden Forces of the Enemy stand guard at these moments. (If you'd like to get an infographic on the map of how everything works together, go to AlterEgoEffect.com /resources.)

French critic Charles Du Bos once said, "The important thing is this: to be ready at any moment to sacrifice what we are for what we could become."

The truth of life is, no matter how successful you are, no matter the stratospheres you reach, there are times when you still struggle, when you still feel you're underperforming. Everyone, even the world's most elite athletes and most successful businesspeople, struggles somewhere on their playing field. The ones who succeed are the ones willing to look at their game film or data and get honest about how they're showing up. Sometimes you lack the courage to try, and sometimes you lack the courage to admit you've been trying the wrong things.

Shaun and I took a close look at his past successes and his past failures to see what we could uncover that could make a big difference.

"Of all your activities, is there one that, when you've done it in the past, has created more business opportunities for you?" I asked.

"Yeah, when I host 'lunch-and-learn sessions' at the office and invite prospective accounts and even existing accounts. I'll give them a little presentation about what we're working on, show them the new technology, introduce team members, and answer questions."

"Awesome. So how many of these lunches did you do last year?"

"Uh, I did one."

His answer threw me. "Seriously? It's your most successful activity, and you stopped at one?" I prodded.

He laughed. "Yeah, not the smartest move."

"No judgment," I said. "Obviously, there are reasons why you didn't host more lunches. If you found that one thing that makes a pretty significant difference in your performance and what your boss is judging you on, what stopped you from doing it more?"

Remember in the last chapter, the Five Bridges to Progress? If you look at that previous question, we found a "More of" bridge. I was trying to uncover what Shaun was thinking or feeling about that activity.

"It's the logistics. Scheduling, getting the space booked, ordering the lunch, getting guest passes approved, and on and on," he said. "I just don't like doing all the administrative stuff."

"It sounds like you need some help with project management," I said. So, we got his technology partner at the company on the phone, and he agreed to help out. We opened up Shaun's calendar and scheduled six "lunch-and-learn sessions" over the next ninety days right there on the spot.

Once we cleared that off his plate, we turned to his presentation skills.

"How do you feel about making presentations?"

"I'm a people person, but presenting to these people is tough. They're the most hard-nosed negotiators in business. The finance world is loaded with superstar negotiation specialists. Give me the spotlight, and I'll shine. But I don't feel confident standing in front of my customers, plus the presentations corporate gives us are boring and too detailed. They could be so much better."

Beyond the confidence issue of being in front of a hardscrabble group of business pros, we dug around more and were able to pinpoint what skills and capabilities he fell short on. In his case, I suggested he read the book *Resonate*, by Nancy Duarte, to help build more story-driven presentations. Sometimes you're given tools that aren't optimized for you, so if you can change them, do it. However, sometimes you're just limited to what is being given to you, and that's what your Alter Ego will help you overcome as well. That's just life. None of us gets *every* single resource to succeed; however, it's what you do with what you've got that will be the difference in whether you find yourself in an Ordinary or Extraordinary World.

In Shaun's case, we needed to change the tools he got—presentations—then we worked on creating an Alter Ego who walked in confident, sure of himself, and relaxed and who saw himself as a formidable and influential presenter.

When we started working together, it was near the end of November, and by the end of February, he had hosted five lunch-and-learn meetings, spawning more face-to-face meetings. This not only caused his sales numbers to soar, but he also broke an all-time sales record in February. Traditionally, February is the slowest month in the tech sector. He went from being trapped in his Ordinary World to living in an Extraordinary World as he rose to the top of global sales and began to be asked by the leaders of the company to share his methods to everyone, which only advanced his career and notoriety even more.

He would never have positioned himself to leave the Ordinary World behind if he hadn't focused on his Moments of Impact and identified the precise behaviors and actions he needed to change to get new results.

DIFFERENT MOMENTS OF IMPACT

My Moments of Impact are different than yours, just as they are different than Julia's. Julia owns a Web and creative agency in Phoenix,

Arizona. With a team of eight, her squad is the driving force between interior design, bloggers, and online influencers. By her admission, she'd been struggling to grow her business and to become more visible and dominant in her space, not because she didn't have the skills, but because something internal was getting in the way.

Her Moment of Impact occurs during client negotiations. "I want to please everyone," she says. "I want to say yes to everything. But then I get myself into a huge heap of trouble because, sometimes, what I've promised isn't doable on the back end. Or I end up in a cycle where I have to let people down because I overpromised."

During her Moment of Impact, Julia doesn't stand her ground; she doesn't stand up for what she believes or wants. She falls back into people pleasing, which keeps her stuck underperforming.

"I've heard it since my teenage years, and when I started my business: 'Julia, you're too soft. People are going to walk all over you, and you're not going to get anywhere.'"

But as she explained to me, she doesn't believe she's too soft. "I'm incredibly ambitious and determined on the inside, but that's not showing on the outside."

Julia is like a lot of people. She has the skills and capabilities. She's been incredibly successful in her chosen path, but it's also been a grind. She's had to fight against some powerful internal obstacles to get to where she is.

On her business Field of Play, when she's negotiating with clients, instead of being strong and assertive in that Moment of Impact, she kowtows. She's too sweet, too accommodating, and she lets clients walk all over her. She overcommits and overpromises, although, deep down, she knows she shouldn't. Her Heroic Self isn't coming forward, and, as a result, her business isn't growing the way she wants it to.

She came to me because she wasn't consistently acting like the leader she knew she could be.

RECOGNIZING YOUR MOMENT OF IMPACT

Your Moment of Impact comes down to knowing what outcomes you're supposed to create on your Field of Play. What are the traits, capabilities, skills, attitudes, beliefs, values, and all the other bits and pieces that you need to succeed?

Just like Shaun and Julia, you have a Moment of Impact that drove you to pick up this book. Something is happening, some behavior and action you're taking—or not—in your Moment of Impact that's influencing the results and creating an Ordinary World.

We have to find not only your Moment of Impact, but the precise behaviors and actions you're taking, or not, that are causing you to come up short.

Are administrative tasks like Shaun's your Moments of Impact? Probably not. They're responsibilities, but they're not going to catapult your career in unimaginable ways, like, say, delivering a killer presentation in front of your boss. Those tasks were the obstacles to his Moment of Impact.

What you're looking for are those moments that will give you the highest rate of return, or the moments that hold the opportunity to provide you the highest percentage of return.

You're looking for those Moments of Impact where you sometimes bring your Heroic Self, but not nearly enough of the time. If you could show up differently, you'd get a different result.

You're not going to concern yourself right now with moments you don't struggle with, even though they might be essential to your success.

As I shared earlier in the book, I started using an Alter Ego in my business life because I was always concerned with what people thought of me. I was so hyperconcerned with my image in other people's eyes that it caused me to be a person I didn't like. Now I'm entirely indifferent to how I come across when I meet people for the first time. I know that I'll treat people with kindness and respect just because it's the right thing to do, and not because I'm trying to get them to like me. If someone doesn't like me, fine. If they do, fine. It won't affect who I'll be or my self-assessment. Some people, when they meet a leader they view as more important, will stumble over their words. Instead of earning a new friend or making a business connection, they become fanboys or fangirls and turn that person off.

One of Julia's Moments of Impact was during client negotiations. One of Shaun's was account presentations. Early in my career, my Moment of Impact happened when I met with prospective clients. I felt like I stuttered and stumbled and came off as too indecisive and insecure to close the sale.

Here are three everyday Moments of Impact. Use them as inspiration to find yours. (If you'd like to get a more extensive breakdown across different worlds like sports, business, and personal life, go to AlterEgoEffect.com/moi.)

Delivering presentations or speaking publicly. Sweaty palms, short breaths, nervous tics, and jumbled sentences greet countless people. They know they can't avoid having to give a presentation at a staff meeting, or they realize that to up their online business, they need to start hosting more webinars or training seminars. I work with quite a few people who struggle in this Moment of Impact, which, when they underperform, can significantly handicap their careers. You need to seem more than comfortable in the spotlight; people want to see public speakers who seem born to do this. This is true whether you find yourself in the corporate boardroom, on a stage at an event, or during a team meeting.

I also see a variation of this when some people get so nervous or are so insecure—doubting, worrying, or judging—about their abilities and contributions that instead of sharing their thoughts and ideas in a meeting, they remain silent.

Networking or meeting someone for the first time. Some people, when they walk into an event, become wallflowers. They only talk with the people they know, or they seem so uncomfortable that they come across as nervous and awkward. Other people kick into overdrive and zip around a room spitting business cards out to everyone who makes eye contact with them. I've worked with people who mow through an entire room, laying waste to it and missing real opportunities to connect with people in meaningful ways. Meeting and connecting with people remains one of the critical ways we grow our businesses and careers.

Closing a sale. There are times when someone signals that they're ready to buy a product or service. Sadly, the seller is too busy following their sequence or process, so they miss him or her. They act like robots instead of displaying flexibility and behaving like a human. People can get hung up on asking someone else for money, and they end up fumbling with the conversation. They'll keep talking, and I've seen them unsell. Or they never close the sale because they come across as too insecure or too timid.

WHAT'S YOUR MOMENT OF IMPACT?

If you apply the Five Bridges of Progress to the Action Layer, you'll want to apply these two elements of the framework:

- Stop doing/stop holding back/stop avoiding/stop behaving/stop choosing
- Do less of/choose less of

Remember, the Action Layer contains your actions, reactions, behaviors, skills, and knowledge. It's all the capabilities you're bringing to your Field of Play. How are you showing up? How are you acting?

How are you behaving? What choices are you making? If you pass all those questions over the bridges of Stop and Less of, you may find some key things preventing you from achieving what you want.

This is about looking at the Action Layer of the Field of Play Model to investigate how it might be affecting your results. Just like in your Ordinary World, be clear with your answers. Be precise. Be descriptive about what's happening or not happening during your Moment of Impact.

Remember, you're gathering all the data right now. Later, you'll build an Alter Ego who will show up in a different way—possibly the opposite way—from what's happening right now in your Ordinary World.

If you need to, go back to the last chapter and see what you wrote. You may have discovered your Moment of Impact when you described your Ordinary World. Activate or stay trapped, those are our only options.

With the work you've just done, you may be getting a lot clearer about how you're going to be showing up on your Field of Play and the new results waiting for you. Why? Because, to ensure we've explored your entire world, we're going to shine a light on what's been driving this performance—or underperformance. Up until now, you've had this thing lurking in the shadows, preventing your Heroic Self, with all your capabilities, skills, and talents, from coming forth. It's operated and acted in the shadows, cloaked in secrecy, but not for much longer—because now it's time to shine a light on the Enemy.

CHAPTER 6

THE HIDDEN FORCES
OF THE ENEMY

The coach on the other end of the phone was getting more agitated and finally yelled into his phone, "She *should* be winning major championships, but instead, she blows these matches she could be easily winning! I just don't get it!"

After talking to the coach for about fifteen minutes, we agreed I would be a good fit to become a part of the team. Rachel is an incredibly talented tennis player who handily dominates her opponents early in the match. But she struggles to hold on to the big leads and momentum she builds. To the armchair analyst, it would look like she loses all the gas in her tank and can't finish. Her play sputters out, and her opponents can often come from behind for the victory.

When I met with Rachel for the first time, and I ran her through the mental game and performance assessment, it wasn't clear exactly why there was this conflict between what she was capable of and how she was performing. It only became clear because of a BLT sandwich.

Rachel and I were sitting down at one of my favorite comfort food places in Manhattan, Penelope's, on the East Side. It's a tiny place with great food and one of the best BLTs you'll ever have. She was passing through New York for a media event, and we discussed her training, the upcoming season, and life in general. When the bill came, I reached for it, but she snatched it quicker than the flap of a bee's wings.

"This one's mine. You got the last one."

"No, no, no," I said. "I invited you out for lunch. Those are the rules. The invited never has to pay."

"You can get the next one. It's only fair."

Boom! It all clicked. This insignificant back-and-forth finally made all the puzzle pieces fit together.

I explained this earlier, but it's such an important concept that I'm going to repeat it: We exist on multiple Fields of Play. The home field, the sports field, the friends field, the work/career field, the hobby field, the health and wellness field, and so forth. On each of these fields, we're called to take on different roles. Each role has a different set of requirements. My dad role and my professional role are very different. Just like my sporting role and my spouse role are different. Those are all different fields or stages you enter and perform on, and they demand different parts of yourself to show up and be great.

We're showing up as different versions of ourselves all the time. This is natural, and it's human. Right now, you may be bringing a version of yourself with specific qualities and traits to your Field of Play and in a Moment of Impact that isn't serving you. It isn't positioning you to succeed, let alone live, in an Extraordinary World, which is where you'd love to be.

So, who or what is influencing this version of you showing up in the Ordinary World?

Inside the world of the Alter Ego Effect we call it the Enemy.

The Enemy is a force creating inner conflict and stopping you from showing up as your Heroic Self. Since the beginning of time, humans have talked about this phenomenon. Carl Jung called this the Shadow. In *Star Wars*, it was the Dark Side of the Force. To mythologist Joseph Campbell it was the dragons that needed slaying.

I assure you, the Enemy is nothing new, strange, or unnatural. It isn't something to hate or beat yourself up over, although we're typi-cally *very* good at doing that to ourselves.

Life is a duality. It's about opposites. Light and dark. Birth and death. Up and down. Inside and outside. Day and night. Yin and yang. The natural world is filled with duality, and you're a part of that natural or-der, too. What you've been fighting—the Enemy—is actually a natural part of how you're built.

And, oh, by the way, it has to be there.

For there to be light, there has to be dark. For there to be up, there has to be down. For there to be the Hero, there has to be the Enemy. It's about balance.

And while the Enemy is a part of you, it's not *you*.

The Enemy is not only about the worry and judgment you fear from others; it's also a blending of certain beliefs and values, and the spe-cific traits—skills, capabilities, behaviors—that are getting magnified and trapping you from taking the action you want.

The Enemy is the source of those unwanted behaviors and actions that I had you identify in the last chapter. Whether you're meek during a negotiation, whether you pass the ball or don't pass it enough, whether you refuse to volunteer to lead a project or say yes to too many things, that's the force of the Enemy trapping you. The Enemy is stealing your moment from you, and keeping you tucked away, safe and sound, in the Ordinary World.

THE COMMON FORCES

The Enemy hides in the shadows, pulling, twisting, and wielding what I call Common Forces. It creates a cascading effect of negative thoughts, emotions, and behaviors that impact, and explain, how and why we show up and underperform on our Field of Play or in a Mo-ment of Impact.

The Common Forces that can hold us back from achieving our goals are things like:

- Not controlling our emotions
- Lacking self-confidence
- Worrying about what others may think of us
- Doubting our abilities
- Taking more risks in life
- Not being intentional
- A bad attitude

When you think back to the Field of Play Model [Figure 3.5], the Enemy likes to use these forces at any of the layers.

- Worrying and feeling anxious about your Field of Play and the people on it; your boss, your coach, your opponent, the market, home field, the pressure of the situation.
- Doubting whether you have the skills, abilities, resources, or grit to make it happen. To pull it off. To win.
- Lacking the self-confidence to show up and perform at your best, despite the fact you do have the skills.
- Concerning yourself with the risks of trying something new and possibly failing at it, even if it's a small step.

You end up rationalizing that it's easier to play it safe, because you won't get fired or cut from the team. However, your True Self feels the sting of not taking the chance.

Having a bad attitude can become a way to excuse yourself from trying harder, from overcoming the resistance and fundamentally making yourself feel safe. Have you ever told yourself you don't need to practice today? That it's okay to be lazy today, and you'll work twice as hard tomorrow?

The only reason I call these common is that they're the forces you would most commonly talk about among friends, teammates, family, and peers. The example I gave about me punching someone on the volleyball court out of anger is a good example of not being able to control my emotions. There wasn't some deeper reason lurking in the shadows. It was just plain ol' immaturity and lack of emotional control. The simple fact that these are obvious forces doesn't make them any less troublesome. However, as you'll find out, an Alter Ego can more easily overcome these types of forces.

The only Common Force I haven't mentioned yet is not being "intentional," and that's because it's not often discussed. However, it is common to the lack of results most people are getting. The power of thinking in terms of Fields of Play allows you to be deliberate and intentional with who is showing up, which is one of the great benefits of having an Alter Ego. The problem that arises when someone isn't being intentional is that they can carry aspects of their personality onto the Field of Play that are not suited for the activity. I'll be getting deeper into this force throughout the book as we create your Alter Ego. I'll also show you how it affected Rachel, the tennis player, later in the chapter.

The human mind is a powerful factory able to produce any number of powerful images and emotions that can either help or hurt your cause.

"You're not ready for that promotion. You've never managed people before."

"Are you sure you want to spend that much on an investment property? That's a big risk and you've only ever done smaller deals."

"Don't take the shot, what will everyone think if you miss it?"

"Mary is a better chef than you and even she doesn't have her own restaurant. Why do you think you'll be able to open a restaurant?"

"You should probably let Charlie be the captain. He's a better
   leader."
"You're starting your business too late in life. You should've done
   this years ago. You missed your opportunity."
"You're not very good at doing sales pitches, so you'll probably
   have a tough time raising money."
"Your new marketing strategy sucks!"

Do any of these statements sound familiar? The Enemy will use
these worries, doubts, and confidence busters to prevent any chance
of you showing up as you truly can. I worked with a basketball player
who struggled to stop worrying about what his parents, and the fans
in the stand, thought of his play. He became so wrapped up in what
other people thought of him that he struggled to settle into a rhythm
and made a lot of mistakes because his head wasn't in the game.
The fact is, he's one of thousands I've seen worry about what others
thought.

As a CFO for a consulting firm, Karen's biggest struggle was giving
presentations. As an executive, this was a major part of her job. It
didn't matter that her information and analysis were on point, or that
she's always one of the sharpest and brightest minds in the room. She
doubted herself.

The statement "I can't give presentations" was a loop in her mind
before, during, and after the presentation. When she would stand
before a group, her nerves and anxiety were visible. Her voice would
sometimes crack, and when asked a question, she would stutter, stumble, and ramble, in the most painful ways.

She didn't just judge herself; she was also plagued by worries that
other people were judging her, which created a vicious cycle that per-
petuated the belief that she wasn't an excellent presenter.

I've found that most people have the skills and knowledge already
available to them to transform their results, Karen did, and she found

an Alter Ego to beat the Enemy and step into being a great presenter. The Enemy is sneakily using the forces to concoct a persuasive argument against you, preventing you from taking action, like starting that business or going after the promotion.

By the way, I'm not advocating for people to pretend they have highly technical skills without doing the work. If you want to be a cardiothoracic surgeon, you need advanced degrees and years of schooling and experience before you're ready to step into that role. But when you do step into that role, you need to bring your A game 100 percent of the time.

While those are the Common Forces that can slow you down or stop you, there are Hidden Forces that are harder to detect and can control your life like strings on a puppet. They come in the form of:

1. Imposter syndrome
2. Personal trauma
3. Narratives

HIDDEN FORCE 1: IMPOSTER SYNDROME

When I started working with Dave, he had already started and grown a thriving business selling software products. He had gained a significant amount of traction in the market, and he was ready to scale and expand. To do that, he needed to move into the corporate space where he had room to grow. He didn't have a steady enough cash flow to fund the next growth stage, so, for the first time, he was searching for investors—venture capitalists, to be exact. With his track record of success, it was easy for him to land multiple meetings with some high-profile VCs.

You would think that everything was aligned for Dave, and it was.

Except, Dave wasn't aligned with Dave.

Instead of swaggering into those meetings, he crept into them like a dog with its tail tucked between its legs. It's no shock to learn he wasn't getting the responses he had hoped for. That's when he came to me.

After I had talked to Dave for a while, it became obvious he was a smart, competent, and accomplished person. However, Dave didn't see himself as accomplished. He basically dismissed away a lot of his achievements and hard work as "luck" or "right place, right time," and he plainly didn't believe he belonged with these other venture capitalists.

What afflicted Dave is a force called imposter syndrome. Many high achievers and successful people struggle with it. If your Enemy is throwing imposter syndrome at you, you can take some solace in the company you're keeping. People like Albert Einstein, Maya Angelou, John Steinbeck, and Tina Fey—to name a few—were or are all highly accomplished people who have spoken or written about feeling like a fraud.

When the Enemy rears up in the form of imposter syndrome, it will whisper a sinister narrative into your ear, spinning a story that your success is more about luck or serendipity or your genes than hard work. It causes people to dismiss their skills and capabilities or previous wins. Imposter syndrome is one of the most insidious little rots that can influence your behaviors and the actions you take on your Field of Play.

Steve Jobs said, "You can't connect the dots looking forward; you can only connect them looking backward."

This is what the Enemy will do to explain away our achievements and success. It connects all the dots that came before in a logical sequence and spins a compelling narrative that downplays and dismisses our hard work and accomplishments.

"Yeah, well, I was in the right place at the right time," the Enemy will say. "Of course, I won an award. I've been doing this a long time, and it was inevitable. I'd be a loser if I didn't win something by now."

Or the force of imposter syndrome will rationalize, "It's not that big a deal—a lot of other people have done it."

There's just no owning any success you achieve and stacking it in your win column. The force just won't let it happen.

What happens when imposter syndrome has you in its grip? You become terrified you'll be found out. Despite all her acclaim and success, this is what Maya Angelou feared. "I have written 11 books, but each time I think, 'Uh-oh, they're going to find out now. I've run a game on everybody, and they're going to find me out.'"[1] You might be surprised to find out how many accomplished people think to themselves they'll be "found out," then ostracized and ridiculed. However, it's irrational. It would only happen if you actually *did* have no skill, no ability, or no knowledge, but that isn't the case for most people.

This is the ultimate fear, isn't it? Being found out and kicked out of our tribe? By nature, we're tribal. Humans survived through the millennia because we were part of a tribe that hunted, gathered, sheltered, and protected one another from the elements, from predators, and from other tribes. You couldn't be out hunting and watching the fire simultaneously. You needed other people if you had any hope of surviving through the night. If your tribe finds out you're a fraud, it triggers that primordial "Uh-oh, they're going to kick me out! I'm going to be caught in the wilderness alone!"

When plagued by imposter syndrome, people don't take themselves, their abilities, or their accomplishments seriously. If you don't take yourself seriously on any Field of Play, you most likely won't be getting the results you want.

HIDDEN FORCE 2: PERSONAL TRAUMA

Some people have lived tough lives. They've lived through very traumatic events. It could have been living through a war or the death of a parent. It could have been the conditions they grew up in, like poverty, an abusive home, discrimination, if they were teased as kids, if they had a health issue, or if they lived through some other event that left an impression within them.

Friedrich Nietzsche once wrote, "To live is to suffer, to survive is to find some meaning in the suffering."

You can't heal emotional scars with an Alter Ego. However, you don't need to carry that weight with you everywhere you go. Not to ever dismiss away traumas, but the stories the Enemy tells us about ourselves, about those events that we experienced, often don't serve us. The Enemy will blame you for bringing it on yourself, or tell you people with your past can't overcome it. That story spinning inside is coming from the Enemy.

Take Javier, for example. Javier is a soccer player whose coach believed the best way to motivate his players was to yell and scream at them. For some of the men, it was what they needed. For Javier, not so much. Javier's father was an alcoholic, and he ran his home and his children like a drill sergeant. His father was an imposing man with a frightening temper, who ruled through fear.

Whenever Javier's coach yelled, instead of it being an injection of motivating energy, it triggered an emotional reaction connected to his personal history. Suddenly those feelings of terror surfaced. Javier's past was getting in the way and causing his emotions to kick into overdrive and create a lot of mistakes and make a lot of fouls.

To be clear, your personal history isn't the Enemy. The Enemy only uses past traumas against you if it can. People have things happen to them all the time that they would never want, but they use them to fuel their success. Later in the book, you'll meet people who have used past traumas as fuel by changing the meaning of those events. Or they've created an Alter Ego from the ground up that doesn't battle with that history and can finally show up as they desire.

HIDDEN FORCE 3: TRIBAL NARRATIVES

This is one of the more powerful forces because it affects your thinking and behavior on your Field of Play from the Core Drivers. These are the deeper things you connect yourself to and the unconscious beliefs you've adopted because of prevailing narratives. The Enemy is sneaky. It slips in unnoticed and attaches itself to stories about what a certain group of people can or can't do. It creates beliefs about who is worthy of achieving something, which you may have unwittingly adopted and now color the way you see the world and what's possible.

If I grew up with a family narrative that said, "Hermans don't have money" or "Hermans are average people," then that thought and belief would impact my behavior, my performance, and my ideas of what's possible.

The Enemy, as a tribal narrative, can also be around your family. It's the narrative your family has told for generations. "We're not entrepreneurs" is something I hear from a lot of my business clients who are, often, the first ones in their families to start a business. Is this story true? No. Anyone can be an entrepreneur. But their Enemy is weaving a tale based on their history and what they've experienced, and it's affecting the self that's showing up.

A fantastic example of someone challenging the status quo is dancer Misty Copeland. She's an accomplished ballet dancer now and the first African American to be named principal dancer at the famed American Ballet Theater. However, as she was developing as a dancer, there wasn't anyone who looked like her at the highest levels. Not only was she African American in a predominantly white classical dance world, she was also more muscular than the classical petite frame the ballet world was used to. Fast-forward to today and she's now a celebrated ballerina for the American Ballet Theatre, performing on the biggest stages and in front of thousands of fans. She could have easily succumbed to the Enemy telling her African Americans don't belong in that world. However, she chose differently and has inspired a whole new group of girls to dream big.

I mentioned the need to be a part of a tribe when explaining the force of imposter syndrome. It's in our DNA. Imagine you were living like a caveman, with saber-toothed tigers and woolly mammoths roaming the land. Imagine you got booted from your tribe. You'd be on your own, forced to hunt, clothe yourself, and find shelter on your own. Who would protect you?

We still cling to that desire to fit in, to find our tribes and be accepted by them.

One of the most influential tribes we're a part of is our family. I've seen many people battle the expectations of their family or the beliefs about what it means to be a good family member. And it's prevented them from leading the lives they've wanted. I come from a family that's incredibly close. My two brothers, sister, and my parents all live near my family's farm in Alberta, a farm that's been in our family for generations.

I wish I lived closer to them and my kids could know and be around their cousins more. I wish I could see my family more often. But I made conscious choices to build a life elsewhere. I chose New York City because I knew it would afford me more opportunities for career and professional growth. Even today, decades after leaving home, I still feel the Enemy pull this string every so often. I still hear that nagging voice questioning why I left, and what kind of son or brother leaves.

Too often, the Enemy causes us to become so concerned with upsetting the people closest to us that it impacts our decisions. It causes us to make choices counter to what's in the best interest of our careers, creative endeavors, and what we truly want.

I can't tell you the number of people who, when we start to examine what's going on, turn out to be afraid of showing up as a Heroic Self. Why? Because they're afraid of success, and it causing them to leave their Ordinary World and enter their Extraordinary World, where their friends and family may not accept their new reality. They'll find themselves wandering in a desolate land, alone and lonely with nobody there to support them.

During an online training event, I was coaching a professor at New York University who previously taught at the University of North Carolina and Stanford. For six years he'd been building a business on how to create better cultures aimed at business leaders. He created a formula and curriculum, and he was eager to work with companies in the New York metro area. He sees his Extraordinary World clearly, but he hasn't been able to take that first step from the Ordinary to the Extraordinary.

"With a full-time teaching schedule at the university and the launch of this training company, I just don't have the time. And I can't go and hire someone to go and help me with this," he began to tell me.

I stopped him. "Wait, why can't you go and hire someone?"

"Because if the professors in my discipline find out that I was getting someone else to research this program, then they're going to ridicule me."

"How do you know that's true? Will they?"

"Well—" he began, but I cut him short.

"You realize that this is what stops most university professors who've got smart stuff that their clients and customers would truly benefit from? You realize these thoughts and beliefs are what prevent people like you from ever launching something out into the broader world? You're thinking and worried about what all the other professors, the people in your tribe, think of you. But who cares what they think? They're not the people paying your paycheck. They're not the people who stand to benefit from your ideas and solutions."

He just sat there staring at me.

Almost every one of us is looking for approval from our peers, from the people we see and believe are our tribe.

What about you? Does the third force trap you in any way? Family and peers are only a couple of the ways this Enemy can keep you trapped. There are cultural, religious, racial, and gender-specific ideas people have rattling around in their heads, too.

"That's only for those people. If I did that, my people would think I'm a sellout."

"The people at my church/mosque/synagogue wouldn't like it if I did that."

"Only men can do that."

"Only women can do that."

"I'm great at math and science, so I should be a doctor or engineer."

"Canadians are nice and never argue." (I had to slip that one in there.)

The point is, there are many ways the Enemy pushes you back from taking action on your goals and causes you to choose to stay trapped. But not for long . . .

What happened to Rachel?

Remember Rachel from earlier in the chapter? What was causing her to fall short on her Field of Play, the court? Why did the BLT sandwich suddenly make me realize what was causing the Enemy to show up on the court?

It was simple: she valued fairness. Rachel is one of the sweetest, most kindhearted people I've ever met. However, when someone would cut in line at a coffee shop, it would drive her crazy. If she saw a homeless person on the street, she'd give them whatever she had to make their day more comfortable. She was extremely charitable.

So you think, Great! How could that be a problem!? We need more people like that.

I agree; however, there's a time and a place for everything, and sports or competition isn't the Field of Play for being charitable.

I immediately called her on it and said, "Rachel, I think I've finally cracked the nut on you."

As we walked out the doors to the restaurant and stood on the corner of 31st Street and Lexington Avenue to talk, she said, "What do you mean?"

So I asked, "When you start beating someone handily and get way up on them, what do you start thinking or feeling about the other person?"

After a little back-and-forth to get clarity, she thought for a moment and said, "Do you really have to beat her so badly? Don't rub it in too much and make her look bad. Do you have to rub it in that you're better than her? Are you trying to embarrass her like some show-off? I would hate to lose this bad."

"And then what happens?"

"That's when I let up."

"Exactly. And that's because you're bringing 'Everyday Life Rachel' onto the court. The Rachel that values fairness and all people being treated equally. And it's causing you to let up. The only fairness that matters on the court is that you play by the rules of the sport, *not* whether or not you need to let someone lose by only a few points. There are winners and losers in competition, and your role is to give it your best and see which side you fall on.

"And right now you're the one that's deciding someone shouldn't have the experience of 'embarrassment, humiliation, or failure,' and you're robbing them of the opportunity to improve. Because those experiences often create the catalyst for change for someone, and *that's* not fair. You're giving them a false sense of how good they are. You need to use every ounce of your skill on that court, and if that ends up smashing someone, great! You've just given them a gift."

She stood there for a moment, with taxis whizzing by and people rushing by us on the sidewalk, and finally said, "I never thought of it that way. It makes so much sense! The 'Everyday Rachel' has a purpose and the 'Court Rachel' needs a persona custom-fitted to that environment."

"Precisely."

There's nothing wrong with valuing equality. Except, in the world of sports and competition, there's no place for it—sportsmanship, sure, but someone has to lose. Fairness was such a core part of who she was that Rachel brought it with her onto the court, and it just sabotaged her performance.

With Rachel, I never tried to talk her out of valuing fairness, nor did I tell her she needs to change her value. Instead, we created an Alter Ego who didn't carry her definition of fairness onto the Field of Play. Rachel's Alter Ego instead valued fierce competition and winning with honor—like a true champion sportswoman.

So getting back to the Enemy's forces, if you're not clear about what or who needs to be showing up on your Field of Play, you can end up carrying a Trapped Self onto that field that won't serve you.

In the previous chapters, we used two of the Five Bridges of Progress, Stop and Less of, at the Field of Play Layer and Action Layer of the model. Now it's about applying this framework to the Belief Layer and Core Drivers Layer to reveal any blocks and reveal any forces affecting your results. What do you want to:

- Stop believing/stop thinking/stop valuing/stop projecting/stop judging/stop carrying the weight of some tribal narrative
- Feel less of/think less of/worry less of/doubt less of

If you think about any of the Common or Hidden Forces, you could apply the "stop" or "less of" framework to any of them.

Over these last few chapters, this act of identifying all the things you want to "Stop, Less of," in the way we "thought, felt, acted, or experienced" helped you get to this point, where you can get clear about the Enemy and what might be currently "trapping" you in the Ordinary. Without this clarity, it's hard to build a powerful Alter Ego, because you won't fully understand the "vision" or "why" behind it.

That is why the "fake it till you make it" philosophy has fallen flat for so many people.

"Faking it" until you're "making it" always carries with it the wrong intention. However, having a clear vision created from a deep desire for what you want in an Extraordinary World Activates a Heroic Self, something you feel truly represents who you are and what you're capable of achieving or creating.

Conversely, the Trapped Self is only considered trapped because when you look at the results you're currently getting and who is showing up, it doesn't feel like the real you. Jung called it the Shadow; we call it the Enemy. And as I've shown with previous examples, it can be as simple as selecting the wrong traits to use at the wrong times. It's like the cowboy who brings a knife to a gunfight.

On a different Field of Play, this version of yourself may be the best version you could bring forth, just like Rachel and her fantastic quality of valuing fairness. It's a bit of a mind bender, for sure, but it's also what enables thinking about life through the lens of varying Fields of Play.

BECOMING YOUR OWN COACH

As a performance and mental game coach, my job is to hold up a mirror to the athletes and leaders I'm working with. My job is to get them to see their behaviors and understand the driving force behind how and why they're showing up in their Moments of Impact.

What you've just done is take a closer look at each of the forces so that you can hold up your own mirror. For some people, this may feel slightly uncomfortable. Whenever I'm uncomfortable, I remind myself this is like reviewing game tape. Athletes watch film from practices and games to dissect their form and to find the areas they need to perfect and practice to ensure they show up as their best selves.

That's all you're doing right now with these forces. You're looking at game tape, collecting intel, and gaining greater insight into why you may be showing up the way you are right now.

You may want to read back through the forces and be curious. Adopt an air of discovery. Think to yourself, Hmm, that's interesting. Allow yourself to be surprised by what you uncover. These suggestions involve using the intrinsic motivators inherent in all of us to look at your world with a better mindset.

Sometimes the forces may overlap. You may read through the list going, "Yup, I got that one, and that one, oh, and I definitely have that one, too." You may find that only one resonates with you. You may even discover nothing hits. If you find yourself saying, "Todd, I don't know where my thoughts, emotions, and behaviors are coming from," that's okay. Sometimes there isn't a Common or Hidden Force at work. Don't spend too much time rummaging around inside the dark cavern. If it's not there, it's not there.

Be your own coach, and you'll do just fine. Never forget: the Alter Ego Effect is something you inherently already know how to do. What if I asked you, what would Batman do? Or Ellen DeGeneres? Or James Bond? You'd automatically know how to play with the idea. Maybe not flawlessly, but you'd be able to play with those Alter Egos and show up slightly differently. With this book, I'm just giving you more depth and firepower to turn this into an extremely powerful force for change.

So, if you're ready, let's put one last label on this Enemy.

CHAPTER 7

PULLING THE ENEMY FROM THE SHADOWS

In 2009, Valeria Kuznetsova was a young, rising star in the tennis world. She grew up in a small, rural town, Kalynivka, outside of Kiev, Ukraine. Her little village was like most other small towns that dotted the Ukrainian countryside except for one significant difference, which affected Valeria profoundly. It was filled with nothing but boys.

And they were relentless.

Her older brother, Dmitry, tried to shield her from the teasing, but even he got in on it sometimes, too. They'd tease her about being a girl, about her skinny frame, and about pretty much anything. The worst of it was when they wouldn't let her play their games. No soccer because she was little . . . No basketball because she was too weak . . . No rugby because . . . she was a girl.

Not to be discouraged, she'd fight her way into the games anyway. Then she'd make a mistake and they'd banish her from the field or court.

One day after yet another expulsion from a game, she ran home crying to her *tato* (dad) and shouted to him, "The boys were being mean again!" He got up from his chair, walked over to the closet, grabbed a tennis racket and ball, handed it to her, and said, "Go out back and hit that ball against the garage a hundred times."

Angry that he wasn't going to help her yell at the boys, she snatched the racket and ball out of his hand, stomped outside, and began smashing the ball into the side of the house, muttering under her breath how much she hated Vlad, Sergey, Alexander, Sasha, and especially Igor, the meanest of the bunch.

Twelve years later, she had transformed herself into one of the top up-and-coming tennis players in the world. She used that anger, humiliation, and rage to rocket herself through the tennis ranks and into the elite of the sport. But there was a problem.

When I got the call from her coach to come out to Flushing Meadows in Queens, New York, there was a panic in his voice. He knew he had this great talent in front of him, but he saw her melting into her mental distress any time she began making unforced errors or mistakes.

When I arrived, Valeria was getting ready to start her match against a much lower-ranked player. The match started off with Valeria overpowering her opponent, but then, as we say in the sports world, "the wheels came off." The moment she started making even minor mistakes, you could see her pace and mutter under her breath. And the more the mistakes piled up, the more agitated and animated she'd get.

After the match was over, which she managed to win, we met back at her hotel for a "chat," to see if we'd be a good fit.

I asked her about what she was saying to herself when she was pacing the baseline.

Her first reaction was a look of surprise, then embarrassment. "You could see that? You could see me talking to myself?"

I chuckled and said, "Of course. But don't think it's a bad thing. We all talk to ourselves; it's just a matter of how constructive that conversation is to our ability to perform and do better."

Multiple studies have been done on the power of talking to yourself, and in fact it improves your performance. A study published in *Adolescence* in 1994, titled "Private Speech in Adolescents," showed that narrating the process of what you're doing improves your performance. However, there's another side of the equation.

What happens when your self-talk isn't so positive?

Valeria went on to tell me how she would say things like:

"Get in the game."
"Use your head."
"Stop forcing it."
"Stop being so stupid."
"Not this again."

Or she would ask herself questions like:

"What are you doing?!"
"Why are you letting her back in the game?!"
"Why can't you just settle down?"

Maybe you can relate.

You see, Valeria had fallen into the trap of having a "circular bullying conversation" in her head, what I call the "merry-go-round effect." A conversation that goes nowhere, beats yourself up, and only spirals you into more and more self-defeating chatter.

However, because our minds love to create a story and make us the hero of it, the solution is to give yourself an Enemy to talk to when those seeds of negative self-talk show up.

We go from an internal merry-go-round of negativity to a constructive back-and-forth allowing us to shove the Enemy to the sidelines.

When I explained this nuance to Valeria, she immediately relaxed, tipped her head back, and said, "Igor," with gritted teeth. Then she explained her entire backstory to me, about where she grew up, the boys in town, and all the verbal barbs they threw her way. And how she stood at the side of her family's house, smashing the ball into the side of it, muttering the names of her bullies under her breath.

Igor became the label she placed on the "forces" the Enemy would use to try to "trap" her and pull her into an Ordinary World by getting her angry or frustrated. Instead of adding more emotion to her already intense personality, we took Igor, shrank that negative self-talk down to the size of an annoying pest of an eight-year-old bully, and shoved him to the sidelines.

Valeria's anger and intensity had gotten her into the pros, but it was going to keep her from winning championships. She was going to burn out. So we flipped what had now become a Hidden Force (past history) hurting her performance, and dealt with it by shrinking its size.

Naming your Enemy creates a compelling distinction between the two worlds living inside all of us. The Ordinary and the Extraordinary. It allows your Heroic Self to talk back to the Enemy trying to trap you.

THE PROBLEM WITH THE UNSEEN AND UNNAMED

When you think about the scariest movies you've ever seen, was the killer or monster revealed immediately? Probably not. Because when something lurks in the shadows, when you can't see, touch, or hold it, it becomes more frightening. It's unknown. And when something is unknown, it's difficult to deal with because your imagination runs wild, building it up to be larger than it is. The proverbial "monster under the bed."

Take the movie *Jaws*, for example. Originally, Steven Spielberg intended the huge mechanical shark to play a far more significant role in the film. But it broke, so he and his crew had to use other tricks to build the suspense. Remember the music? A deep beat begins to build . . . You know something is coming, something from the vast depths beneath the water . . . but you don't know when or where or whom it will strike.

No one saw the shark. You just see a girl splashing around, and then suddenly getting pulled under the water. Talk about terrifying! By not seeing the Enemy, Spielberg knew that he would trigger our imaginations to run wild.

The imagination is a powerful tool, which we'll intentionally use to build your Alter Ego. But like all great tools, it can be wielded for positive or negative results. Sometimes your imagination, when not adequately harnessed or controlled, will run amok filling in and creating an even more terrifying story. "How big is this thing? I don't know, but it must be huge!"

The more something remains in the shadows, in the dark, unseen and untouched, the scarier it becomes.

In the last section, we began to shine a light on the Enemy and its forces. Now I want you to drag it from the shadows and give it a name.

That's right, I want you to name your Enemy.

As soon as you give something a name, you've given it an identity. You've given it a form, a shape, a structure. When we give something a shape, we are also giving our Alter Ego something to defeat, something to overcome, something to battle against.

Let me show you what I mean. When I say the names the Joker, Darth Vader, or even Saddam Hussein, what did you see? I bet a picture instantaneously popped into your head, as automatic as breathing, and along with that image or thought, you may have even felt a specific emotion.

This is the power of giving something a name. Giving it a name, and giving it a form, allows you to talk to the Enemy, get it off your Field of Play, and give it a swift kick to the sidelines (I'll show you how later in the book).

You can choose any name.

A lot of this depends on your personality and what makes sense to you. You can make it silly. Make it scary. Make it something that ignites your anger or rage. Or something that used to scare you but doesn't anymore, like Valeria did with Igor. Or simply give it a plain ol' name like Michael, Sara, Jesse, Tony, or Hans.

A word of caution around an Enemy that brings on anger and rage. These can be great focusers for athletes. I've had Olympians and pro athletes channel rage during competition and then play with it beautifully. Unlike a lot of self-help books that preach peace and tranquility as the pathway to performance, I tell people that rage and anger can activate peak performance. However, make sure they suit *your* Field of Play.

The bottom line: Make it something you're going to love facing down and conquering.

What do I mean? Humiliate it. Make the Enemy as small as possible. Make it cute. Make it something that you'll look at and go, "Aw, aren't you adorable." Take away all its fear over you. Make it the most nonthreatening thing you've ever seen. Make it a puppy and call it Scooby-Doo. Call it Fluffy or Pippi. Only make it Darth Vader if it's to remember that Darth Vader is a bald actor in an uncomfortable suit.

Now, if you're someone who thrives on conflict, who needs a challenge in life to test your mettle and bring out your grit, then do the opposite. Make the Enemy fierce. Make it scary. Make it intense. Pick the name of your childhood bully, or a boss you detested. Pick a family member who has tried to hold you back or told you you'd never amount to anything. I've even had clients pick a parent as their Enemy.

Truly, anything goes.

Whether you make the Enemy funny, silly, harmless, or intimidating, scary or challenging, give it a name. It makes it easier for your imagination to give it form and substance. You can also pick a character from a book, television show, movie, or comic in which someone else has gone through the trouble of developing lots of details about this person. You're looking to get as detailed as you can so that it will make visualizing the Enemy easier for you. The more vivid your Enemy, the easier it will be for your Alter Ego to drive it from your Moment of Impact.

If you decide to pick something like an animal, you could simply use "wolf." Or give the wolf a name, like "Cristobal." It's the difference between saying, "Hey, Wolf! Step to the sidelines, because you don't want this fight," and saying, "Hey, Cristobal! This is my time. I'm not ruled by you anymore. Bugger off!"

IF YOU'RE STUCK ON A NAME . . .

If you can't figure out what to name your Enemy right now, wait.

Many clients have to build their Alter Ego first, and then they pick something or someone that is their Alter Ego's natural Enemy. They'll also pick something and name it someone they know without a doubt their Alter Ego can and will easily defeat.

So, if you aren't inspired right now, wait and then come back. Build your Alter Ego's origin story, then fill in the Enemy's name. Get all the way to the Response Proclamation and then come back.

Remember, there's no "perfect" order to any of this. You name the Enemy when the Enemy is clear to you.

CHAPTER 8

THE POWER OF YOUR STORY

After my presentation to a room filled with Army Green Berets and Rangers, I walked off the two-foot-high stage to greet a few people with questions for me. After I had talked to a few of the rangers about superheroes and comic book villains, a colonel tapped me on the shoulder and asked me if we could have a private conversation. I said, "Of course." Together, we walked out of the auditorium at the Fort Bragg military base in North Carolina, the world's largest military installation.

Fort Bragg is home to the United States Army Special Operations Command, which is responsible for training, equipping, and deploying special forces around the world for their various missions. Judging by the lines around the colonel's eyes, I was facing a hardened professional who had spent a lot of time squinting through binoculars or the scope of a gun and could tell me stories for days.

"First, I want to thank you for coming and spending some time with our men and women; we appreciate it," he started.

The one thing I've always appreciated about speaking to military crowds, whether they're elite Navy SEALs or fresh-faced recruits, is that everyone is extremely gracious to a civilian like me, and they always refer to a larger "we."

"It's always an honor to come and share and hopefully make a difference," I said.

"You said something interesting in there that I wanted to discuss with you."

"Sure."

"You mentioned the meaning of the uniform we all wear. And how different uniforms mean different things, and if we're not careful, those meanings can either help us or hurt us. I realized something at that moment. This uniform isn't helping me."

"What do you mean?" I asked.

"When I put this thing on, it means something to me. I love wearing the flag on my sleeve, I love serving, and I love training these men and women. Which means I have to be tough, challenging, and strong. We talk about honor, code, and the chain of command all the time. But I just realized it's been hurting my kids.

"Every day I get home and the kids want to spend time with me, and I immediately start grilling them about homework and chores. Even after I get changed out of my uniform, I'm still the same person. I've been racking my brain for the past twenty minutes trying to figure out how to apply what you talked about."

"Colonel, since the founding of the nation, the military has been building a history, story, and credo of what it means to wear that uniform. Are there handbooks everywhere on the base about what it means to be in the U.S. Army?"

"Yes."

"Well, your story is pretty similar to what most people around you tell themselves about the uniform, give or take a few details. It's re-inforced through repetition and an environment built to support it. But where on the base or anywhere else, for that matter, do you go to get your 'dad' uniform? Where's the handbook about the history, story, and credo of what it means to join the brotherhood of fatherhood?

"When you go home and change out of your uniform, do your jeans and golf shirt 'mean' anything to you? Probably not."

When you pay attention, you realize you're a natural storytelling machine. Every day, you're telling yourself a story in your head, filled with a colorful narrative about life. You're also listening to other people tell you their personal stories, and you're sucking up story after story from social media to television to print. In her book *Wired for Story*, Lisa Kron dissects the latest in brain science to teach writers how to tell stories that pull their readers in and keep them flipping the pages. As Kron explains, "We think in story. It's hardwired in our brain. It's how we make strategic sense of the otherwise overwhelming world around us."[1]

Right now, whether you realize it or not, you're living out a powerful story. Sometimes it's a story you've created over time, telling yourself why you can/can't, do/don't, or should/shouldn't show up in a particular way on the many Fields of Play of your life. Other times there are potent narratives built into the world you live in, just like the colonel. They're often ideas we've unconsciously adopted from any of the Core Drivers Layer, which could be family, religion, country, gender, race, or a group you're a part of. Occasionally we become slave to a story we didn't even realize we accepted.

What do you think of when you see the following words?

Shy	Investing
Saleswoman	Cooking
Fistfight	Flying
Clutch player	Long lines
Gossip	Winner
Scientist	

When you saw the word *shy*, did you automatically think of its literal definition, "nervous or timid in the company of other people," from the *Oxford Dictionary Online*?

Or did you think of someone you know who's shy, or did you think of an entirely different meaning or story around the word *shy*?

What about the other words?

We all have reactions to different words, either positive, negative, or indifferent. I was talking with an entrepreneur who told me, "I really want to grow my network, but I avoid people and social situations because I'm shy and introverted."

The story she told herself was, "Only outgoing, extroverted people are good at meeting people. Shy and introverted people can't." The problem: I know a ton of "shy" and "introverted" people who are outstanding at networking. Yes, there was a part of herself that was shy and introverted, but being shy and introverted aren't negatives unless you make them negatives. She was losing out in her business world because she wasn't showing up with confidence. To succeed, she needed to cease being shy about selling her products and services.

She needed to stop telling herself a story that said, "I am shy and introverted, so I can't network."

Now, here's one of the benefits of the Alter Ego Effect: instead of trying to go on the long road of "changing herself," she could step into an Alter Ego that isn't shy. This bypasses a Common Force that prevents people from achieving their goals, being more intentional about who needs to show up.

These narratives or stories we're telling ourselves are important because unconscious ideas and emotion drive action. Each of us is driven more by our gut feelings than our thoughts. Marketers and advertisers deeply understand the connection that emotion has on driving our actions to buy a product or service to satisfy a want.

These masters of emotion know that the fastest way to get someone to buy from them is to tell a compelling story. Seth Godin, one of the leading thinkers on marketing, says, "The reason all successful marketers tell stories is that consumers insist on it. Consumers are used to telling stories to themselves and telling stories to each other, and it's just natural to buy stuff from someone who's telling us a story."[2]

Godin's book *All Marketers Are Liars* discusses the idea that "[e]very-one is a liar."[3] Godin writes, "We tell ourselves stories that can't possibly be true but *believing* those stories allows us to function" (emphasis added).[4]

There is perhaps no faster way to evoke a strong emotion than to tell or hear a compelling story. We feel stories, and when we feel stories, whether we're feeling fear, anxiety, joy, or happiness, those emotions can prompt us to act. When we're telling ourselves powerful negative stories, wrapped up in a Hidden Force, then they become self-fulfilling prophecies.

Imagine for a moment that five minutes before a big meeting with a prospective client, a script began playing internally. The script went like this: "I'll never close this prospective client. He's way more successful than me. I don't have anything worth selling. They're so much better than me. I'm such an imposter. They're going to realize I don't belong in this room with them."

When that's the story you're telling yourself about *you*, it's pretty hard to walk into that meeting, relaxed, confident, and self-assured that you have an incredible opportunity to offer the person across from you, and they'd be lucky to work with a partner like you. You're crossing wires. It's challenging to tell such a demoralizing story and then go out and rock it.

This happened to Jimmy, a sales rep for a large national insurance company. He came up to me at a conference because he was frustrated that he kept missing his quarterly numbers. His boss was riding him hard, and Jimmy feared that if he didn't get those numbers up, he'd be canned. As a young father of three, with a mortgage, he was understandably stressed.

When we dug deeper, I discovered he hated making sales calls—which is pretty tough, when that's your job.

"Why do you hate making sales calls?" I asked.

Jimmy shrugged and said, "I'm uncomfortable making them. I don't know what to say. People always seem too busy to talk. They're just hard."

"Okay, well, when you think of a salesperson, what image pops into your head?" I asked.

"Someone annoying or bothering someone," he shot back.

"Interesting. What about them is 'bothersome or annoying'?"

"People know that you're there to get their money."

"So, when you think of a salesperson, you imagine someone out for themselves?"

"Yes."

Jimmy didn't know it, but he was acting out an incredibly potent story. This story was rooted in a deeply held belief about salespeople. "Salespeople are dishonest. They don't care about people. They only feed people lines so they can nail the sale," was the story. No wonder he hated making sales calls and failed to meet his quarterly numbers. Every time he picked up the phone, the Trapped Self that showed up hated salespeople. This is one of the Common Forces I outlined in chapter 6, "a bad attitude."

There was no way his Heroic Self, with its best traits, was going to shine through. He could have tried to change his behaviors and actions, he could have tried to tell himself that salespeople are fantastic (which they are!), but it probably wouldn't have stuck. Not when the Trapped Self he brought to his Field of Play categorically believed salespeople weren't to be trusted.

Jimmy wasn't showing up with confidence, integrity, or passion on his calls. Every time he picked up the phone, the little tape in his head played: "Hey, Jimmy, what makes you think these people want to talk to you? You're just out to hustle them for money, aren't you? You're not fooling anyone. They see right through you. Come on; they have better things to do with their days. Wrap up this call—now!"

Imagine how much more successful Jimmy's calls would have gone if he picked up that phone and the story he acted out went like, "I can't wait to talk with Bob and find out if there's any way I can make his life easier, better, or more enjoyable."

If that was the story Jimmy believed, I guarantee he'd show up differently, with more confidence and conviction, smoothly closing more sales. I bet he'd have a lot more fun, too.

If you're furrowing your brow, shaking your head, or pondering what story or stories in your head are influencing your results, don't worry. Often the Enemy, the forces, and the story we're living out can be a part of one big tangled web trapping us.

I've teased these three threads apart, not so you can tie yourself up and get frustrated or overwhelmed. I've walked you through these areas to help you possibly find some insights into what makes you tick. What might trap you or create unneeded friction?

A BETTER STORY AWAITS

For years Amy worked in corporate America in project management and strategic planning. She had followed her dream of starting a business, and, like many new entrepreneurs, found her business limping along. When I connected with Amy, she was a year and a half into her new business and struggling with a widespread affliction: she had half-finished bridges. She started a lot of projects but couldn't drive them to completion.

"I told myself that I was a 'total starter, a nonfinisher.' I never finished anything, so no wonder I wasn't getting the results," Amy told me. "I told myself this story for thirty-eight years, and it created so much suffering. Suffering from missed opportunities, from the crippling self-doubt, of the self-judgment, of the self-criticism."

When I introduced the Alter Ego concept to Amy, who is now an entrepreneur, it made sense to her immediately. "I was in a place where I was open to hearing new things about myself, and about the way that I thought about myself, so I was able to notice all the talking that I was doing to myself, and the stories I was telling myself. My current story was, 'I'm inconsistent with my results, whether that was related to my health and wellness, my relationships, or my business.'"

The story Amy had lived for so long was that she was "inconsistent with the results in her life." Her Alter Ego's story became the opposite. Her Alter Ego's story was "I'm consistent with the results in my life."

"I never thought I could be different," Amy said. "I could just choose to decide to be different, and that was available to me. I had no idea! I thought the story that 'I'm inconsistent' was a fundamental part of who I am, and that I could never get rid of it. I journaled about this for years! And then, all of a sudden, this story didn't have to define me. I could write a new one, and I could be different."

Amy's story and the others before her reveal that when you use the creative force from your Core Self and intentionally decide who will show up, the things and behaviors you've "always had" can shift instantly. As I said in chapter 5, on your Field of Play and in your Moments of Impact you have all these traits available to you. But most of us don't realize it. Most of us don't realize that we can choose to magnify different characteristics in different Moments of Impact. Most of us don't realize that we're telling ourselves a lethal story that we believe is gospel when, in fact, we can silence it and create and live a new story.

In the last few chapters, we looked at the Ordinary World and how the Enemy, Common and Hidden Forces, and personal narratives have a powerful effect on how or if you show up as your Heroic Self.

Tell me . . . are you willing to have a little fun? Are you willing to use the power of your imagination and play with a natural part of the human experience?

Are you willing to suspend who you've been and how you've performed for a moment in time, and let another version of yourself show up instead?

When I first started working with a mentor of mine, Harvey Dorfman, I marveled at his indifference to the opinions of others. It made sense that one of the preeminent mental game coaches on the planet didn't worry about the judgments of others. But it still amazed me, mostly because it was the very thing crippling me from taking action. Now the need to be validated by others has long gone, and it still amazes my wife that I once struggled with it.

When I was in my early twenties, I was a lot different. I was so concerned about the opinions of others that I allowed myself to play second fiddle to everyone. I put everyone else's needs, wants, and desires above my own. I cared so much about what other people thought of me and whether they liked me that it held me back.

The only place where all bets were off and I could suspend trampling myself and interests was on the sports field. Parts of the identity and behavior of my Alter Ego, Richard, his decisiveness and self-confidence, were borrowed from the sports field. People that I coach tell me they wish they could stop caring and worrying about what other people think of them.

"If I could just tap into that like you do . . ." they often say.

They can, and so can you.

For a moment in time, just a few minutes even, anyone can suspend the stories they've been carrying with them on the Field of Play and in a Moment of Impact. Anyone can overcome whatever Hidden Force is holding them back or change whatever story they've been living out.

All it takes is your willingness to suspend your disbelief.

After I asked the colonel about his dad uniform of golf shirt and jeans and whether it meant anything to him, he struggled with the idea that it could mean anything significant. But just as I assured him, I want to assure you; there's a natural process you already use that can turn something ordinary into something extraordinary.

CHAPTER 9

CHOOSING YOUR
EXTRAORDINARY WORLD

Twenty-one years ago, I met a man who was doing what I wanted to do. When I was growing up as a farm kid, 4-H was a natural part of the process of living in the farming world. 4-H is like agricultural Boy Scouts. You select which "club" you want to join—cattle, horses, sewing, etc.—and you spend the next year working on a project. I was in the cattle club. And from the age of ten, I would go out into the pasture with my dad, pick a young male calf or steer, take care of it for the next eight months, wake up early to feed it, and come home from school and head straight to the barn to feed it again. I spent parts of weekends training it to be led around on a halter. This effort culminated in all the "cattle clubs" from our area "showing" their "steers" at a final competition.

By the way, 4-H stands for "Head, Heart, Hands, and Health," and it's meant to develop character, responsibility, and leadership. Beyond caring for my steer, which I typically named Brutus, Barney, or Bam because I felt *B* was the appropriate letter to start a young steer's name with, we also had to take part in creating a governing body for our club. We elected a president, vice president, treasurer, and secretary. The purpose was to teach governance and learn how to run an organization with professionalism. We also had to prepare and give a speech about any topic we were interested in at a yearly competition.

This is the part you may cringe at. Having to stand up in front of your peers, parents, judges, and a room filled with sixty to two hundred people is enough for most people to recoil from. And it was, for everyone else—except me. I loved it. I loved the process of writing my speech and having the chance to give it. At the age of ten, I won the competition, competing against kids a lot older than I. Ironically—because of the career I ended up pursuing—my speech was about the Olympics.

Now, this isn't a story about how amazing I am, by any stretch, because in many ways the deck was stacked in my favor. I was around parents who often had to give presentations or speeches, and I was an outgoing kid who loved the spotlight, so being on a stage wasn't a big deal to me. However, it gets us back to that man I mentioned at the beginning of the chapter.

I went to an event with my uncle in the Rocky Mountains of Canada where he was receiving an award. I sat next to a man at the head table who was different. He asked questions to a twenty-one-year-old that I hadn't been asked before.

"So, what do you feel called to go and do?"

"What do you want to be proud you accomplished by the time you're thirty?"

"What's the biggest action you could take in the next two weeks that will help you move toward that goal?"

It was refreshing. Having an older gentleman take that much interest and causing me to think differently was a new experience. He seemed wise, refined, and genuinely interested. I told him about speaking as a young kid and how I wanted to find a way to do that as a profession. About owning my own business and traveling the world because I hadn't seen much at the time.

The conversation flowed until it was interrupted when they introduced the night's keynote speaker. Suddenly the man I was talking to got up from his seat and went to the podium. I felt like an idiot. I just got done telling this man that I wanted to speak for a living, essentially, and he was the actual speaker for the evening. Over the next fifty-three minutes, I sat spellbound. He was incredible.

He said things like:

"Whatever good things we build, end up building us."

"If you don't like how things are, change them! You're not a tree."

"We must all suffer one of two things: the pain of discipline or the pain of regret."

Jim Rohn was the most eloquent wordsmith I'd ever heard. *Forbes* magazine even named him one of the three most important business philosophers of the twentieth century.

When he sat back down after a standing ovation, and I pulled my jaw up from the floor, I apologized for not knowing who he was. He shot back, "Apology accepted," with a wink.

After that night we ended up staying in touch, and he became my first mentor whether he liked it or not. But about eighteen months into knowing Jim, we were talking on the phone one afternoon and I shared with him the struggles I was running into trying to grow my sports training business. He replied with a line I'd heard him say in different ways before, but this time it landed very differently. He said, "Todd, if you're not willing to risk the unusual, you'll have to settle for the ordinary."

GETTING OUT OF THE ORDINARY AND INTO THE ZONE

I've mentioned the Extraordinary World and what awaits you when you escape the forces that pull you into the Ordinary World. But the Extraordinary World isn't unicorns, gumdrops, and prancing fairies. The Extraordinary is filled with challenges, obstacles, and dragons to slay as well. And that's both the journey and the reward.

"So many of us choose our path out of fear disguised as practicality. What we really want seems impossibly out of reach and ridiculous to expect, so we never dare to ask the universe for it," said actor and co-median Jim Carrey when he gave the commencement address for the Maharishi University of Management in 2014.[1]

Instead of asking the universe for it, I'm saying, build an Alter Ego that will go on a quest to attain what you want. "I learned many great lessons from my father—not the least of which is that *you can fail at what you don't want, so you might as well take a chance on doing what you love* [emphasis added]," Carrey added in his speech.[2]

The Extraordinary versus the Ordinary is filled with more meaning, more intention, and more possibility. After twenty-one-plus years of working with elite people on the Fields of Play of sports, business, and entertainment, I've learned every single one battled an Enemy pulling them into an Ordinary World. Every single one had an excuse, reason, or personal story they could easily lean on to shy away from the challenge of their chosen pursuit. Except they didn't. Many of them stepped into an Alter Ego to make it happen.

Even Cary Grant once said, "I pretended to be somebody I wanted to be until finally, I became that person. Or he became me."

Those challenges, forces, obstacles, and dragons that need to be slain, however big or small, are already there whether you like it or not. And instead of just pumping up my clients or motivating them, we used an Alter Ego instead. Just like tennis superstar Rafael Nadal, Beyoncé, David Bowie, Bo Jackson, and thousands of other people accomplishing amazing things, you can use the Alter Ego to shield your Core Self and absorb the arrows, barbs, or worries you've imagined in your mind will happen if you act in any way different from your personal narrative and story you've told yourself of *who you are*.

NFL running back Jay Ajayi is known for being calm, cool, and quiet off the field, and he explained his Alter Ego "Jay-Train" this way: "I think some players, that's just how you try to get in your zone where everything is instinct, and you're just out there playing the game. For me, it's the Jay-Train."[3]

The pursuit of finding "flow state" or "getting into the zone" has been the core focus of the work I've always done with athletes, entertainers, or professionals. When you reach this place, performance is heightened; it's improved.[4] It's this intoxicating place where time seemingly stands still, where capabilities flow through you without thought, and you have this sense of just observing yourself perform. It's incredible.

However, the challenge in training people to find that place was like trying to thread a rope through the eye of a needle. Why? Because fundamentally, most people, even the best of the best, get affected by the Common or Hidden Forces or try to "control the outcome" rather than trusting themselves and the process.

An Alter Ego can help build intention, promote belief, and create trust.

The famous poet John Milton once wrote, "The mind is its own place, and in itself can make a heaven of hell, a hell of heaven."

The power to change lives inside us.

Imagine you're one of my clients competing at the recent Olympic games in South Korea, in an alpine skiing event. You're waiting atop the mountain at the starting gate, clipped into your two-meter-long skis, staring down a course that looks like a vertical cliff covered in patches of ice, waiting for the signal to burst through the gate. You'll be racing at speeds that would pass a car on the highway, and the only thing stopping you from crashing into the pine trees is an orange plastic fence.

Sound dangerous? Absolutely. Should you be thinking about that danger, imagine falling, catching an edge, slipping on the ice, or getting tangled in a pole as you race by? Hell no.

If you're a skier and you're at the starting gate with seeds of doubt starting to sprout regarding the windspeed, the conditions on the hill, whether or not you can beat the time that Svetlana from Slovenia just put up, then you've been pulled back into your Ordinary World. There's no trust. There's no zone or flow state. And there's no personal-best performance, either.

This is what happened to Ian when he fell behind during tennis matches. "I'd start losing, and then I'd think, How am I going to come back? What's losing going to feel like? What am I going to tell my parents? What am I going to tell my friends? What am I going to tell my teammates? Guess what happens when you get in that place? You lose," Ian told me.

WHY DOES ALL THIS MATTER?

Renowned researcher and author on human performance Steven Kotler explained how using our imaginations taps into the creative part of our mind and short-circuits the negative self-talk and criticism the Enemy likes to use. Studies have shown that negative self-talk, doubt, and disparagement go quiet when we're engaged in creative work.[5]

An ambitious entrepreneur, Alonto is a great example of the creative force in action. He's had dreams of leading thousands of people as a proud Filipino American, and the first time he had the chance to get onto a stage was in front of seven hundred people. Except Alonto didn't get on the stage. It was Big Wave, his Pacific Islander Alter Ego, who showed up, influenced by the Maui character that Dwayne "the Rock" Johnson plays in the movie *Moana*. "I was nervous as hell right beforehand, freaking out, and sweating. The first time I stepped in front of the audience and took on the Big Wave persona, everything else fell into place. I don't even know where the words were coming from. It was almost like I was being given the words just by having the faith that I could step into that leadership role."

Whatever Field of Play or Moment of Impact you're creating an

Alter Ego for, I want you to have the same experience Alonto and thousands of others have found using this process. You want to imagine how your Alter Ego will act, behave, think, speak, feel, and perform on that Field of Play. Then, when it's time for your "phone booth moment," you'll intuitively know how to perform. And the likelihood of kicking open the metal gate to the zone, flow state, or Extraordinary World will have just improved.

WALKING THE BRIDGES FROM OUTSIDE TO INSIDE

The question people are most challenged with answering:

"What do I want?"

The blank look I see people give me is a common one. It's like they're scared to admit what they want. Even successful people can struggle with this question. However, a mindset accomplished people use to routinely achieve their goals is "end-in-mind" thinking, meaning they have a clear idea of what target they're aiming at, where they're going, or what they're creating.

Lucky for you and me, there's more than one way to get there.

I leaned back in my chair, waiting for Michael, a fairly successful real estate professional, to answer my question: "What do you want?"

He looked pained, like he couldn't see it or admit it. So I interrupted his mental traffic jam and asked, "What *don't* you want?"

Immediately, with a lot of frustration and emotion he unleashed a flood of don'ts:

"I don't want to worry about rejection anymore."
"I don't want to worry about what my boss will say if I don't hit my numbers."
"I don't want to wake up dreading my day anymore."
"I don't want to feel like I'm wasting my days away."

He rattled off twelve more don'ts before he stopped to catch his breath.

Just like Michael, it's so much easier for you to create a Don't Want list, which is exactly what you did when you unpacked all the layers on the Field of Play Model. [Figure 9.1] However, now it's time for your "Want List." So, if you actually went on the internal quest to reveal those things, now it's time to get clear about your Extraordinary World.

Now, before you fall into the trap of an internal dialogue like—

"Who am I to ask for what I want?"

"I'm not supposed to want or to have more than others."

"I sound so egotistical."

—here's what I'd like to say to that: "Sound egotistical."

Admitting you want something isn't egotistical. It's honest.

FIELD OF PLAY MODEL

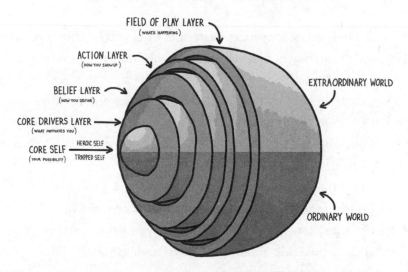

Now, just as we've used the Five Bridges framework in previous chapters, we'll be applying them to your Extraordinary World, and the first place to start is with your ideal results on your chosen Field of Play and then we work our way through the layers to your Core Drivers.

If you recall, the Five Bridges consist of Stop, Less of, Continue, More of, and Start. Except in this quest you'll only be using three of those bridges: Continue, More of, and Start. You're shifting your "orientation" on the Field of Play Model and shifting your intentions to something positive, which leverages the "self-expansive" or "Wow Mindset," which changes your motivations to the things you'd like to gain, not lose or avoid.[6]

To begin the process of getting clear about your goals, outcomes, or results we'll start with your Field of Play, what would you like to:

- Continue experiencing/continue getting as a result/continue achieving
- Experience more of/get more of/achieve more of
- Start experiencing/start achieving/start getting

To make it easier for you, these results would all be things you could hear, see, taste, touch, or smell. For example, maybe you want to:

- Continue hearing the positive feedback on your creative work
- Continue seeing your revenues grow
- Continue seeing the reactions people have of your cooking/painting/writing/design work, etc.
- Continue tasting your recipes improve
- Continue smelling the aromas of the place you live
- Continue touching the quality tools you get to work with
- Hear people talk about or share your ideas more
- Score more during a game
- Get more interviews
- Win more awards
- Receive more referrals

- Have more income
- Make more sales calls
- Make more pars and birdies as a golfer
- Attend more networking events and engage with more people
- Work out more
- Start a new career
- Start seeing your creative work displayed publicly
- Start owning more real estate
- Start traveling overseas and experiencing new cultures
- Start getting scholarship offers
- Start hearing scouts talk about you
- Start getting more press about your work
- Start seeing your investments grow
- Start living someplace new

I'll bet if you look at your Field of Play, there are already some positives you can continue developing. The bottom line when getting clear about this area is that everything is tangible. The Field of Play is where your results exist. Now, as you move on to the Action Layer, you want to think about the actions, behaviors, and skills your Alter Ego will use to help make those outcomes happen. The questions to ask yourself are, what do you want to:

- Start doing/start responding/start behaving/start choosing/start saying/start thinking/start attempting
- Do more of/choose more of/behave more like/say more of/think more of/attempt more of
- Continue doing/continue choosing/continue thinking/continue behaving/continue saying/continue attempting

The Action Layer contains your actions, reactions, behaviors, skills, and knowledge. It's all the capabilities that you're bringing to your

Field of Play. How are you showing up? How are you acting? How are you behaving? What choices are you making? If you pass all those questions over the bridges of Starting, Continuing, and More of, you'll get even more clear about how the "new you" will show up. For me, when I was starting out in business, I wanted to "act more decisively," because I was getting caught up in paralysis from analysis. So maybe you want to:

- Ask for the sale more
- Paint more
- Act more confidently
- Book more meetings
- Walk with my head up and more confident
- Make more eye contact
- Reach out to people more
- Start cooking
- Start writing
- Start playing the guitar
- Start preparing yourself better
- Start planning your week or month more effectively
- Start taking more shots
- Practice more
- Drink more water
- Say "I love you" more
- Smile more
- Launch more product offers
- Meet with team members more
- Attend more conferences
- Invest more money

When you look at this list, which isn't exhaustive, these are all the things you could do to help make the outcomes happen. These are the new actions you could take during those Moments of Impact. In the Ordinary World, these are the actions, thoughts, or behaviors you're not taking or having, leading you to get the results you don't want. (If you'd like an even more exhaustive list of actions you could take, go to AlterEgoEffect.com/resources for more help.)

Once you move through this layer, you want to apply this same framework to your Belief Layer to reveal the new emotions, feelings, qualities, and expectations you'll possess, which makes those actions much easier to execute. This is the new internal experience you'll have as you approach and experience this Field of Play. These are the forces your Alter Ego will use to combat the Common and Hidden Forces with more grace, resilience, and confidence. So, what do you want to:

- Start believing/start expecting/start feeling/start valuing
- Believe more of/expect more of/feel more of/value more of
- Continue believing/continue expecting/continue feeling/continue valuing

Essentially, you're asking yourself what you need to believe to make those actions effortless, joyful, or more comfortable. Also, what do you need to expect about yourself or the Field of Play you're standing on to make those changes happen? And what do you need to value about yourself, the world, the people you interact with, your skills, and your knowledge to feel more confident/decisive/enthusiastic/ peaceful/optimistic, etc.? (For a more exhaustive list of positive emotions to make this easier for you, go to AlterEgoEffect.com/resources.)

Maybe you want to:

- Start valuing action over perfection
- Start feeling more competent
- Start believing you're capable
- Feel more enthusiastic about your progress

- Feel more optimistic about your ability to make a difference
- Expect people to say yes to your ideas
- Expect yourself to continue moving past challenges because of your determination
- Gain more satisfaction from your efforts
- Feel more grateful about the opportunities you're presented with
- Start expecting your shots to go in
- Feel like you're an unstoppable force
- Feel like people want to hear from you
- Expect your art to move people
- Believe the stage wants you on it and feel excited about your performance
- Feel like you're as important as anyone
- Love failing, because you know you're improving and taking action!

Contrary to popular memes and quotes about successful people, that last one is key. Winners become winners because they failed more than others. So why not have a healthy relationship with that experience? It doesn't mean you accept failure as an identity. It simply means you don't let it define you and you know you're gaining more wisdom with every attempt.

Ultimately, this process is going to help you find an Alter Ego that embodies these qualities naturally, so you can step into its power and create a new reality for yourself.

WHAT DOES YOUR EXTRAORDINARY WORLD LOOK LIKE?

Ian, whom I introduced you to earlier in the book, is enjoying a thriving career as a top copywriter and founder of several companies. By most standards, he's a success. But Ian has harbored a goal he's kept buried his entire life, until recently. It was only when he began tapping into and using the Alter Ego that he was ready and willing to admit what he wanted—to be a stand-up comedian.

This is what he wants to pursue. This is his Extraordinary World. He's now setting up his businesses to run without his full-time attention so that he can pursue a comedic career. He's admitting, articulating, and taking action, right now, to pursue a lifelong goal.

He would never have taken these steps if he didn't first admit to himself what it was that he wanted more than anything.

Do you want to be a powerful presenter? Great. Own it. You want to walk into an event and shake hands and greet people with pizzazz and charm? Great. Own it. Do you want to be a calm, assertive, confident leader in the midst of crisis moments? Great. Own it.

Imagine the behaviors and actions that you're taking in your Extraordinary World. How are they different from your Ordinary World? Are you bolder? Are you more thoughtful? Are you more focused? Do you follow through and finish all the projects you start? Are you more articulate, assertive, or active? Are you more relaxed, calmer, or peaceful? Are you more rebellious? Are you more fierce, bold, or adventurous?

What are the traits that show up in your Extraordinary World?

What are your thoughts and feelings? What would you be thinking of your abilities to create an Extraordinary World? How would you be feeling about yourself, the world around you, the people you interact with? What are your predominant emotions? Remember Bo Jackson: his dominant emotion on the football field was a deep certainty that he would destroy anything in his path, and it didn't matter who it would be. He didn't care.

Although you can't control the outcomes and the results in your Extraordinary World, I still want you to imagine what those could look like. Paint a picture in your mind's eye. How does it feel to live in your Extraordinary World? Do you want to be known as a strong leader in your company? Do you want to be someone who speaks up in team meetings and shares her ideas confidently? Do you want to be someone your team turns to for advice and confidence, who leads calmly and assertively through a crisis? Do you want to have a trophy handed to you onstage for "salesperson of the year"? Do you want to overhear your kids saying to each other how "their mom is the best mom"?

STILL GETTING STUCK?

If admitting what you want or what your Extraordinary World looks like remains a stretch, then try this: ask yourself, "What would my Alter Ego admit it wants or expects to hear, see, feel, touch, or smell?"

While you may not have built out your Alter Ego yet, you may have an inkling of what this secret identity may want. Suspend your disbelief for a moment and imagine that your Alter Ego has zero hangups when it comes to articulating what it wants. He/she/it easily and effortlessly admits what it wants. What does your Alter Ego believe it can do? Or create?

CHAPTER 10

THE POWER OF A MISSION

There are a series of small parks along the Hudson River in Manhattan running up the entire length of the island. For an island filled with concrete, pavement, and skyscrapers, it's a needed escape from the hum and noise of city life. Anytime an athlete is coming through town to play against any one of the ten pro sports teams in the area or a business leader I work with is coming to New York for meetings, it's a convenient chance to connect face-to-face. I'll almost always take them for a walk along the Hudson. We walk because, in my experience, humans are more prone to open up when they're moving. Plus the fresh air and exercise never hurt.

On this one occasion, a client connected me with a teammate in his second year in the NHL. After years of always being a go-to guy, Matt was struggling. He'd gone from always being a star to sinking to the bottom of the mediocre-middle on his NHL team. We'd walked about twenty blocks along the water talking about his future and decided to take a break on a bench at the 26th Street pier.

As we sat down, I leaned forward and asked him, "You know how Batman is fighting for 'justice'? I'm curious, what are you fighting for?"

"What do you mean?" he replied.

"Well, for the past twenty minutes it's been like pulling the teeth from a lion trying to get you to tell me what you truly want from your career. And you just got done telling me you feel like you're letting your dreams slip away because you're getting so caught up in your head. So, personally, that would piss me off. The idea that everything I've busted my ass to do to get here is getting tangled up in a web of bullshit, those thoughts in my head would piss me off. So, *why* are you going to start showing up differently? What are you fighting for? Batman fought for justice after witnessing his parents die at the hands of criminals. We all have something we can fight for: justice, honor, fairness, our family, our community, our religion, our name, even our creative talents. So, what about you?"

He sat on the bench leaning forward with his elbows resting on his huge hockey thighs, staring at the passing ferries, and after a long pause said, "Self-respect."

"Why self—" But before I could finish my question he continued. "To show that someone from my Podunk town in Ohio made it. And bring the Stanley Cup back to our crappy little community hockey rink."

"Meh, sounds cliché. I've heard it before," I shot back at him.

"Fuck you." He quickly responded and was superannoyed. "Why would you say that!? I thought you were supposed to help, not put me down."

"Matt, that feeling welling up right now—what is it?"

"Pissed-offness."

"Good. Don't forget it. Because here's what I know: You carry that with you every freaking time you don't play your guts out on the ice. And you direct that 'pissed-offness' at yourself when you don't show up. My job isn't to be your best friend. My job is to help you perform, and sometimes that means challenging you."

You've just admitted what you want. Good. Now, do you feel a strong emotional pull toward what you want? Do you feel so motivated to go on this quest that nothing will stop you, nothing will get in your way? Does it have meaning?

If your answer is no, we have a problem.

Holocaust survivor and celebrated psychiatrist Viktor Frankl once wrote, "Life is never made unbearable by circumstances, but only by lack of meaning and purpose."

When you look at the superheroes in comic books, the great characters in movies and literature, they all seem to be fighting for something bigger than themselves. And even the ones that start out doing good deeds for selfish reasons end up finding deeper meaning in their labors. It gives the effort, struggle, and challenge a higher purpose.

More and more research is piling up that shows the obsession with "happiness" is causing people to feel empty.[1] In a study published in the *Journal of Positive Psychology* in 2013, Roy Baumeister and his colleagues found that people who pursued activities only for personal pleasure lacked a sense of meaning in their lives. Another study, conducted by Steven Cole of the UCLA School of Medicine and Barbara Fredrickson of the University of North Carolina at Chapel Hill, revealed that people who found deeper meaning in their lives had stronger immune systems than those who had a more self-centered approach to life.[2] This suggests that if you want to chase your goals, finding deeper meaning in your efforts will make you stronger, literally.

You need to feel pulled as if you're on a conveyor belt that goes only one way. There's nothing you can do to stop yourself from being drawn into your Extraordinary World. If you lack the strong emotional resonance, or you're indifferent toward your Extraordinary World, then . . . why are you about to go on this journey? Why build an Alter Ego for a world that you kind of, sort of, maybe want to experience?

"The emotions are mechanisms that set the brain's highest-level goals. Once triggered by an event, an emotion triggers the cascade of sub-goals, and sub-sub-goals that we call thinking and acting,"[3] explains Steven Pinker, Harvard professor and one of the world's leading cognitive scientists.

In other words, our emotions drive our actions. It's almost impossible for you to take action toward something you're indifferent to.

Beyond just taking action, the emotional resonance you feel toward what you want, toward why you're creating this Alter Ego, is also your motivation. The word *motivation* comes from the Latin word *motivus*, which means "moving cause."

As a mental strength coach, there's one thing I can't coach people on. That's motivation. I won't touch it. It's one of the few things that no one can coach you on or create for you. It's the X-factor. I can't make an athlete get up at 4 a.m. to run drills or wind sprints. I can't make an entrepreneur want to start and grow a business or to stick with it when they hit the rough patches. I can't make someone want their goal bad enough that they're driven to overcome any and every obstacle, no matter how tough or how high the cost.

In his bestselling book, *How We Decide*, Jonah Lehrer makes the case that rationality depends on emotion. Feeling, not intellect, drives motivation. Lehrer points out, "*Emotion* and *motivation* share the same Latin root, *movere*, which means 'to move.' The world is full of things, and it is our feelings that help us choose among them."

You have to find that motivation within, and very often that motivation comes from feeling so emotionally connected to what we want that nothing else matters. It's the core purpose of our being. We have to go on this quest. We have to enter our Extraordinary World, no matter the cost, no matter the odds, no matter the outcome.

WANTED: STRONG EMOTION

When you break down the motivations of all the great heroes and heroines in comic books, movies, or literature, you find there are mostly four core motivators, and there can often be a blending of two or more:

Trauma
Destiny
Altruism
Self-expression

Trauma is something that lies at the heart of what started Batman's mission. He dedicated himself to fighting crime after seeing his parents murdered. Whether it's righting a wrong, "sticking it to the man," or showing someone who slighted you that you can't be stopped, trauma in any form is one of the most common sources of someone's mission. In many ways, this is what drove Oprah Winfrey. Even her famous quote, "You can't discriminate against the best," reveals her resiliency in the face of discrimination and trauma.

Destiny is what drives Buffy the Vampire Slayer. She discovers she's the "Chosen One"—blessed with supernatural powers to fight demons. She's reluctant at first but finally accepts the challenge. Many ambitious people I've worked with or spoken to over the years explained this similar feeling of being "chosen." They've explained their aspirations felt more like they'd been chosen to pursue them and there wasn't a choice in the matter. They were the ones that "had to find a way to make it happen." Many of us identify with the feeling of assuming great responsibility.

Altruism is one of the core drivers of Wonder Woman. In the 2017 movie, she selflessly tries to save humanity from evil. Altruism can come in the form of activism and wanting to help or serve others because they are forgotten or because of a great love for them. In many ways, this was a core driver of Matt, the young hockey player I mentioned at the beginning of the chapter. He found deep meaning in bringing hope to an area decimated by the shifting American landscape. Countless young athletes who come from single-parent homes find this to be a core motivator and take care of a single parent who sacrificed so much for them to "make it."

Self-expression is a core driver of people motivated by merely wanting to answer the question, "I wonder what I can do/create/find?" Some people are just deeply motivated to uncover "what they're made of" and love the creative, athletic, or scientific process. Leonardo da Vinci, Charles Darwin, the great Wayne Gretzky, and many others can be found here. (Gretzky, though, also had great reverence for the game of hockey and his family, which would evoke altruism, as well.)

When you look at any of these four motivating factors, they all stem from events, situations, or experiences that started these people down their paths. However, eventually they found a deeper meaning to their work. Batman continued on his mission because he liked helping people and fighting for the "little guy." Oprah continued to find more joy in relating to people with a realness and honesty the public hadn't experienced before, which changed people's lives. Buffy continued her fight because she was there to save the people she loved. And Wonder Woman continued to pursue the ideals of fairness and equality while saving humans from evil.

In all of these situations, their real purpose was eventually transformed by the Core Drivers outlined in the Field of Play Model in chapter 3:

- Family
- Community
- Nation
- Religion
- Race
- Gender
- Identifiable Group
- Idea
- Cause

When you begin to attach what you're trying to achieve to something larger than yourself, it delivers a deeper purpose to your mission. And when it comes to feelings, there's no right or wrong answer to what exactly you're feeling. It just needs to be strong. You may not be able to articulate the feeling—words are a clumsy way to describe a sensation. If you feel strongly about what you want, but you can't tell me what you feel, then you're in the clear. Later, you may find the words to articulate it—or not. Words don't matter here. Just the feeling.

Despite what some people in the self-help movement may preach, negative emotions like rage and anger can be incredibly motivating, especially in the beginning, when you're taking a new action and trying to build momentum. Those powerful emotions move us, and that's what you need early on. Most people are stuck sitting on the sidelines while the game of life is happening on the field. Whatever gets you onto the field and gets you moving is all that matters.

Ask yourself, "Why do I want this?" or "Why do I want to make it my Extraordinary World?" or "Why do I want to create an Alter Ego?"

Purpose and emotion are intimately entwined. For example, my family was and still is one of the leading drivers for why I choose to create and grow companies and to work with athletes, business leaders, and entrepreneurs. Since I was a boy, I've felt a deep sense of responsibility and resonance with my family name. The good people in my family fuel me. That's part of my motivation. It's one of the reasons why I want to realize my Extraordinary World.

And notice I said "my Extraordinary World"—not yours, not my dad's, mine. That doesn't mean I'm selfish, because a *huge* part of my world is serving others. However, I'm the one deciding what that world will look like, feel like, and sound like, not somebody else.

Many people I've met or worked with are driven because they want to escape something or someone in their past. They were filled with anger or rage about an experience or the way someone mistreated them. I met a Mexican American businessman at a conference years ago. We hit it off so well we decided to sneak away at lunch. I learned he had accumulated a substantial amount of wealth in his career. He was kind and soft-spoken, rather unassuming, but when he started to talk about his history, a fire sparked in his eyes.

He told me about one of the first times he showed up at a prospective client's home. As he walked up the driveway, someone was leaving, and as the two passed, this person said to him, "Oh, you must be the new gardener, here to trim the hedges."

That one comment was a turning-point moment for him, he told me. The only reason the person thought he was there to trim the hedges was his skin color. He said, "I made a promise to myself that day to be so rich I was going to turn the tables and hire some white guy to be my gardener." He found his emotional resonance, which helped to push him toward and into his Extraordinary World. That became his initial motivating force, but after a while he began to see the impact he was making in his community and the inspiration he'd become to other Mexican Americans, and it became a Core Driver, to keep growing and taking risks.

This is the type of strong emotional resonance that I'm asking you to find and acknowledge. It's the purpose of why you picked up this book in the first place and why you're building your Alter Ego.

Another example is John. John has an impressive family lineage. His grandmother, originally from Europe, came from a royal family forced to flee during World War II. She landed in Mexico and married a general. John comes from a family known for its power and standing. He's a first-generation American and trying to make a name for himself in business. John has great reverence for his family, heritage, and lineage. And he wants to plant the proverbial family flag proudly in a new country and continue the family legacy. This mixture of his Core Drivers of Family, Cause, and Idea is what's fueling him to push past any barriers he's had in the past.

Sometimes the emotional resonance is driven by our family, our communities, or our nation. I had a client who competed in the Olympic Games in London in 2012 who was inspired to be the first person to have her country's flag unfurl as she watched it slowly rise to the ceiling from her place on a podium. Whether her country's national anthem played because she won first place didn't matter. Seeing her country's flag was all she cared about. National pride was a Core Driver that gave her the emotional connection to the Extraordinary World she envisioned.

She never saw it happen, but coming into the event, she was ranked twenty-eighth in the world in her sport. She wasn't even the top-ranked athlete in her country, but she finished fourth at the Olympics and shattered all her previous personal bests.

Sometimes the emotional resonance behind what we want is very individual. We want to be rich. We want to be secure. We want more power. If your "why" is more individualistic, that's okay; it doesn't have to be a grand plan to save humanity, and it doesn't have to be driven by a peaceful, loving, gentle state of being, either. But as the studies I mentioned earlier demonstrate, it has to be deeply meaningful to you. And in most cases these initial motivators end up finding roots in any of the Core Drivers. You're exploring the boundaries of what you can do. The initial motivation of "wanting more money" ends up becoming attached to impact on Family, Community, or Nation. Or it becomes attached to an Idea that leaves you wondering just how much you can create.

Some of the most successful athletes, business executives, and entrepreneurs whom I've worked with were driven toward their Extraordinary World for selfish reasons. And I don't mean selfish in a negative way, either. If this is the emotional resonance that gets you moving, then have at it. Tell me you want to see your name in lights outside of a real estate office. Tell me you want to see your name as the executive chef at a Michelin-starred restaurant. Tell me you want to sell a company for millions of dollars and then take the paperwork and slam it down on your father's kitchen table, telling him, "And you told me I'd never make something of myself? Now look at me, Pops."

A lot of clients, especially entrepreneurs, tell me they want to be of service to or make a difference in the world. If that's the driving emotion within you, if that's why you're building and creating an Alter Ego, then who am I to tell you to find something else?

I don't care what emotion or what purpose sits inside you; it's none of my business. What I do care about is that you're honest with yourself about feeling a strong emotional resonance with what you want and why you want it. That emotion is what's going to get you moving and keep you moving.

When I started out, my wants were very individualistic. Over time, I've found a good chunk of my emotional resonance and purpose comes from wanting to make the largest impact on the most people I possibly can. That's my fuel. That's why I do what I do today.

THE FIVE WHYS

If you have your emotional resonance and it's strong, or you know why you're creating your Alter Ego, then you can skip this section. Move on to the next chapter.

But if you're struggling to get to the emotional core and to connect to why you want what you want, then try using the Five Whys technique. The Five Whys is a problem-solving tool, invented by Sakichi Toyoda, the founder of Toyota Motor Company, in the 1930s, and more formally developed by Taiichi Ohno, a pioneer of the Toyota Production System in the 1950s. The Five Whys helps someone to find and understand the cause of a problem.[4]

It's a relatively simple process, and great to help you figure out what's really motivating you. Here's what you do: ask "Why?" and keep asking until you get to the core, to that place of deep emotional resonance.

For example, I get up at 4:30 a.m. to meet my trainer from 5 to 6:30 a.m. every Monday, Wednesday, and Friday.

Why? Because I want to be in better shape.

Why do I want to be in better shape? Because when I play with my kids, I want to have more energy than they do. A few months ago, I was playing with them when my back got sore and my breathing labored. Ten minutes in and I was exhausted. I had to take a break. I told the kids I needed to stop; I was too tired. Their looks of disappointment gutted me. I didn't want to be that dad who couldn't keep up, who missed out on moments and opportunities to play with them because he wasn't in the best shape.

Okay, I didn't need five "whys" to get to what motivated me; it only took two. And having the goal of keeping up with young children may have been lofty, but I was up for the challenge of wearing them out. So my Core Driver for altering my fitness was found in my family.

Use as many "Why?" questions as you need. And if you continue with this process you'll almost always end up finding it leads to one of the Core Drivers: Family, Community, Nation, Religion, Race, Gender, Identifiable Group, Idea, or Cause. This is like drilling for oil. You keep asking until you discover a "gusher of emotion." You'll know it when you hit it, because the emotion will be strong. Knowing this is what will keep that fire burning when you're tired and sore, and you want to quit or give up. Every high-performing, successful person faces those moments when they doubt whether they should or even want to keep going. They all question whether the sacrifices and choices they're making matter.

The ones who keep going are the ones who know *why* they're in this race in the first place. They know their purpose for going after their Extraordinary World and building an Alter Ego that will help them get there.

So the simple question becomes:

Why do you want to Activate this Heroic Self onto your Field of Play?

Is it because of a deep connection to:

- Family?
- Community?
- Nation?
- Religion?
- Race?
- Gender?
- Identifiable Group?
- Idea?
- Cause?

Or your original motivation could be stemming from something like a hurt, being wronged, creative expression, or a selfish need. But you'll find that as you move forward, you're going to discover a new Core Driver that will sustain you over the long term.

A PSYCHOLOGICAL TRICK

Many people have a difficult time reflecting on their own lives. Scientists refer to it as *self-reflection paradox*. The idea of asking yourself challenging or difficult questions like "what do you want?" or "why do you want something?" can tie you up in a psychological knot. However, there is a helpful technique called *self-distancing*. Two psychologists from the University of Minnesota and University of California, Berkeley, Ethan Kross and Özlem Ayduk, have done thousands of hours of research on the technique and its benefits.[5]

"It is also possible for people to take a step back when thinking about past experiences and reason about them from the perspective of a distanced observer, akin to a fly on the wall," they write.

So to use this psychological trick to your own benefit, one of the most effective ways is to ask yourself: "Why does 'Jane' want to write bestselling novels?" or "What's the purpose of 'Todd's' life?" This third-person language creates an observer-type effect and can allow you to gain perspective on a challenging or difficult question.

This self-distancing technique provides even more evidence to the power of the Alter Ego Effect. The Alter Ego ends up giving you an observer-type advantage that allows you to free yourself from self-talk loops, or emotional spirals. It gives you the opportunity to ask yourself, "What would Wonder Woman do?" or "How would Mother Teresa respond in this situation?" or "Why is Batman going to finish this hard project?"

So when you think about what your Core Drivers are, or you think about the Core Drivers of your Alter Ego, using this self-distancing technique can help you find your answers.

TIME MAKES "WHY?" CLEAR

The more you bring the most powerful version of yourself onto your Field of Play, the more you're going to discover your "why?" Many athletes, writers, entrepreneurs, and other creatives have told me they didn't start their journeys by knowing the answer to "why?" They were just interested in something, or they had some skills, and they were committed to developing. It was more about self-expression, and as their performance improved and their results changed, their passion for it grew. As their passion grew, so did the clarity around "why?"

Sometimes the answer grows from the doing, not from the thinking or feeling.

CHAPTER 11

DEFINING YOUR SUPERPOWERS AND CRAFTING THE NAME

One of the most challenging sports I've ever worked is equestrian, and Lisa was a tough nut to crack . . .

When you think about all the challenging components I'm trying to bring together so that an elite athlete can perform at their best, it's daunting. Aligning the mental, emotional, and physical worlds can feel like herding three cats at once. But in the equestrian world, a factor gets added that only magnifies those three worlds: a horse.

Equestrian is a fascinating collection of different disciplines. There's horse jumping, horse racing, polo, and dressage, to name a few. And the last is what my client Lisa competed in. It's a fascinating sport, because in other sports like soccer, football, basketball, or golf, you don't have a thousand-pound horse underneath you detecting every single subtle movement, feeling, or thought you have.

If you're not familiar with horses, they're one of the most emotionally mature animals on the planet, which is precisely why they're used in therapy and recovery work for people with PTSD, autism, addiction, and many other mental-health-related problems. But it's this hyper-awareness horses have that makes dressage such a challenging sport.

Merriam-Webster defines *dressage* as "the execution by a trained horse of precision movements in response to barely perceptible signals from its rider." Think about that for a moment. "Precision movements" from a thousand-pound animal with acute emotional abilities, coming from "barely perceptible signals from its rider," which means a human being. And we all know human beings are far from perfect. Again, it's the only sport where whatever you're emotionally feeling gets transmuted to the horse. It means that whatever Lisa's emotional state was, her horse would pick up on it and often reflect it in its performance.

The problem Lisa battled was extreme nervousness and anxiety before competitions, and this would show itself in her posture. She'd slouch a bit, hunching her shoulders. It also showed up in the amount of pressure she'd hold the reins with; gripping too tight was like a telephone wire sending a signal straight to the horse that screamed, "I'm not feeling confident right now, and I'm supernervous, so you should be nervous, too!" Her horse, Ricky Bobby, picked up on everything loud and clear, and he would dance around, his posture would be off, and it affected the scores from the judges. After all, the sport is about precision movements during a predefined routine using subtle signals from the rider.

During one of our first conversations I asked Lisa, "Who or what represents total control, total confidence, and real poise?"

After thinking about it for a while, she responded with "Wonder Woman."

She went on to tell me how much she loved Wonder Woman growing up and the classic character Lynda Carter played on television. She explained the golden lasso and how Wonder Woman descended from a tribe of Amazons who rode to battle on horseback. Lisa had this incredibly strong emotional connection to Wonder Woman, plus there was the shared connection to horses, so it became a natural Alter Ego for her to assume every time she climbed into her saddle.

Every superhero has superpowers that help them overcome whatever conflict exists in their worlds. Wonder Woman has powers like super strength, speed, and flight. Spider-Man has intelligence, the ability to cling to walls and ceilings, and the power to zap a spiderweb from his wrists. Aquaman can control the sea, has super strength, and can breathe underwater.

While you won't be leveraging out-of-this-world superpowers, like stopping bullets with a wristband, using a golden lasso to force people to tell the truth, or shooting spiderwebs from your wrists, your mind has an incredible power to unlock resources you already possess through an Alter Ego you can step into. Those bullets being stopped by Wonder Woman could be the bullets of judgment, fear of criticism, or procrastination your Alter Ego deflects to keep moving forward. Just as superheroes only need and use specific superpowers for their worlds, we only need to use specific superpowers, too.

The superpowers my Alter Ego used in business were the powers of confidence, decisiveness, and being articulate. Why? Because they were the very things I was lacking when I started out, and they were the qualities needed to win on my Field of Play. Now, does my dad, who runs a cattle ranch in Canada, need those superpowers? Maybe, but not necessarily. The superpowers I call on to try to be a great father are being playful, adventurous, and funny. Are those the superpowers that you need to use as a parent? Maybe, but not necessarily.

That's the beauty of this process. You define the traits.

The superpowers you select for your Alter Ego will be the ones you need the most to ensure you show up as your Heroic Self on your Field of Play or during a Moment of Impact. When we looked at your Ordinary World, we looked at how you're showing up and who you are right now. We looked at some of the behaviors, thoughts, emotions, actions, beliefs, values, and other traits that were being pulled.

Now it's time to get intentional and to find the traits—the

superpowers—you need your Alter Ego to call upon and use during the Moment of Impact instead.

People will often ask what comes first: the Alter Ego or the Superpowers? Both and neither. It doesn't matter. Some people know immediately who their Alter Ego is. If that's the case, then we work back to look at why someone chose a specific Alter Ego to tease apart all the traits and to deconstruct the Alter Ego's identity—its behaviors and mannerisms, its skills and capabilities, thoughts and emotions, and beliefs and values about itself and the world.

Other times, we start by looking at the Superpowers someone wants to call forth in a Moment of Impact, say, poise, confidence, and assertiveness. Then we'll search for someone or something that represents those traits, and that becomes the Alter Ego.

There's no right or wrong way. While the book is laid out sequentially, the reality of building an Alter Ego is it's more akin to entering doorways into the Extraordinary World. You can bounce around through the various chapters to find inspiration, which will make the other components finally click for you. Take Zach, for example; he was one of the top collegiate hockey players in the country and now plays in the pros. Like many people, he wanted to dive into creating and using an Alter Ego ASAP. We blew through the first few steps, never digging into how he was currently performing, what form his Enemy took, naming his Enemy, or the deeper purpose driving him to build an Alter Ego.

When we first started working together, he was struggling to come up with the puck when battling in the corners. He wanted to fight harder, but he had a bad injury when he was younger when another player checked him from behind, so fear and worry caused him to go into the battle with too much trepidation. When we started talking about how he'd like to battle in the corners, he immediately thought of the Tasmanian Devil, so that's whom he chose as his Alter Ego. He started taking that mindset out onto the ice and began getting better results. However, it wasn't consistent. So we worked back through all the components of building an Alter Ego, to really allow him to resonate and connect with its deeper purpose. In the end, Zach ended up creating a composite Alter Ego, much like my football-playing one.

This book is very much like a Choose Your Own Adventure novel, where you control the order. As long as you go through all the doors (chapters), you'll position your Alter Ego to deliver the most powerful Ground Punch possible—and in the end, that's all I care about.

BUILDING YOUR ALTER EGO'S SUPERPOWERS

When we looked at the Ordinary World, we looked at who you've been showing up as on your Field of Play.

Now we're going to unlock that Heroic Self by creating an Alter Ego from the ground up. If you happen to know who or what your Alter Ego is already and you know its superpowers, then use the next few pages to hone, refine, and strengthen your Alter Ego.

PROMPT 1: START WITH THE SUPERPOWERS

Look for adjectives. How do you want your Alter Ego to show up during your Moment of Impact? Do you want to be decisive, adaptable, flexible, ambitious, kind, extroverted, calm, bright, brash, tough, courageous, dynamic, easygoing, lovable, boisterous?

If you're unsure, try filling in the blank with this question: "I wish I was . . ."

What or who represents the adjectives you selected? Is there someone you associate confidence with? It could be someone who also is on your Field of Play, or maybe it's someone in a different sector, business, or industry whom you admire for their confidence. There's no limit here. There's no right or wrong answer. There's no judgment, either, on what or whom you choose.

All that matters is that you select something or someone that you deeply resonate with. A client of mine, Heidi, used an Alter Ego that is a cross between the fictional television character MacGyver, who's never met a problem he couldn't solve, and Marie Forleo, a New York City–based entrepreneur who hosts a popular Web video show called MarieTV and has a dynamic and creative personality.

Julia, whom you met earlier, struggled to be firm with her clients in negotiations. A self-professed people pleaser, she said yes to everything and everyone even when it didn't serve her. She wanted to stand her ground, to stand up for herself. Tired of being seen as gentle and soft-spoken, she wanted the ambition and determination she felt to shine.

When she first learned about the Alter Ego, she thought she had to do a 180 with her personality. If she was gentle and soft-spoken, then she needed to roar like a lion. There was just one problem: she didn't feel any emotional resonance with a lion. Actually, she did, but it was negative. She didn't feel like a lion, there was no kindred spirit, and it felt like a stretch.

Then she got a birthday card from her husband. On the front was a deer—a stag with horns. She loved deer—in her words, "I'm obsessed." While people litter their Pinterest boards with cats, she has pictures of deer. Her husband also gave her a necklace with an antler on it. "My husband said, 'You are kind and gentle and yet, so strong,' and the combination of all these things really hit home."

Julia found her Alter Ego—it was the stag. "Stags stand their ground, yet they're quiet and gentle. You still don't want to mess with one. They're determined and stubborn."

She uses her Alter Ego to help her stand her ground even in uncomfortable situations. This is the connection you're looking for with whatever you choose.

You don't need to construct a massive world or have eighteen Superpowers. When I created Richard, I used only three Superpowers: having confidence, being decisive, and being articulate. Kisma, an entrepreneur, has three Superpowers, too: being receptive, clear, and open.

If you're still getting stuck with the traits you want to possess to help you show up on your Field of Play as you want, revisit anything you captured back in chapter 4, "Your Ordinary World," and flip the traits holding you back into the opposite. The reason I chose "decisive" as one of my characteristics was that I was indecisive and procrastinating on the things I knew I needed to do to succeed. You can do the same.

PROMPT 2: CHOOSE SOMEONE OR SOMETHING YOU ADMIRE

The second entry point is to start with someone, something, or an animal you already admire, and to ask yourself, "Why?" What is it about this person, thing, or animal you admire? What traits (or Superpowers) do they possess?

If you're drawn toward comic book hero like Superman, Wonder Woman, Batman, Black Panther, Storm, Batwoman, Hulk, Wolverine, or Spider-Man, why? What traits do they have that you admire or appreciate?

Maybe you're pulled toward a historical figure like Abraham Lincoln, Joan of Arc, Cleopatra, Winston Churchill, Marie Curie, Copernicus, Malala, Martin Luther King Jr., or Leonardo da Vinci. Why? What traits do they have that you admire or appreciate?

Perhaps it's a literary character like Jane Eyre, Harry Potter, Captain Ahab, Nancy Drew, Scarlett O'Hara, Casanova, the Count of Monte Cristo, or even Winnie-the-Pooh (yes, really, anything goes) or a fictional character from a movie or television show. Why? What traits do they have that you admire or appreciate?

Maybe it's a celebrity, athlete, reporter, writer, director, or politician. Why? Perhaps it's someone in your family, maybe a grandparent, parent, mentor, or teacher. Why? Maybe it's an animal. Why? Again, what traits do they have that you admire or appreciate?

Are you drawn to a race car, a truck, a train, a knife, a gadget, a gizmo, or something robotic? If you're telling me you know without a doubt that your Alter Ego is an engine that never quits, then who am I to argue? It's your world, and you create your Alter Ego. The key, like with any Secret Identity you're stepping into, is to have a strong emotional connection with it.

Sport is littered with athletes who use machines as an Alter Ego. NFL running backs Jerome "the Bus" Bettis and Jay "the Train" Ajayi are great examples. Both of them love(d) the idea of putting their teams on their backs and carrying them to victory. Or plowing over defenders. A sales rep reached out to me once to tell me he chose a magnet as a part of his Alter Ego, to attract the perfect clients and deals. "My Trapped Self had such a terrible attitude. I felt like everything was just harder for me than others. So I wanted my Alter Ego to experience less resistance and effort to everything I was doing. Mike 'the Magnet' Murphy was born."

You can build an Alter Ego from any source, like:

- TV or movie character
- Literary character
- Cartoon character
- Superhero
- Entertainer
- Historical figure
- Animal
- Machine
- Something abstract
- Athlete
- Someone from your life, like family members, teachers, friends, or mentors

(For a more exhaustive list, along with the traits associated with different characters, visit AlterEgoEffect.com/inspiration.)

Joanne, the lady I mentioned in chapter 3, was born in England and moved to Australia for a few years when she was nineteen years old. She saw this documentary on Tracy Edwards, the British sailor who in 1989 skippered the first all-female crew in the Whitbread Round the World Yacht Race. Joanne deeply connected to Tracy, who as a young girl grew up in a poor, landlocked town.

"There I was, this young girl from Manchester who was going to Southampton University, where all the great yachtsmen go, where they build boats, and where the men are all proper, and the first thing I did was walk into the club and join. I ended up winning the European boat championships twice, but in that moment, I had no idea how to sail, just a determination to learn, like Tracy.

"I decided to embody Tracy Edwards, this woman who I saw as focused, strong, and who surrounded herself with other strong and empowered women. I had never seen that before. Until watching that documentary, I didn't realize I could be female and successful without having to emulate the men."

MaryAnn, who owns the auto repair shop with her husband, found that she was always drawn to animal prints. When she started playing with an Alter Ego, she asked herself, "Why?" Why was she drawn to these prints? "Animals are pure instinct. They don't have imposter syndrome. They're just strong, and they get done what they have to get done," she explains. "Without being aware of this, I gravitated toward that kind of energy—it made me feel more confident and powerful."

PROMPT 3: IT'S RIGHT IN FRONT OF YOU

Is there someone from your past whom you have a connection with or who feels like a kindred spirit?

Two of Julia's Alter Ego's values are adventure and travel. She's drawn to the Austrian Alps, even though she grew up in Germany. Her great-great-great-great-grandfather was an alpine explorer, and there is a museum dedicated to him back in his village. He was a romantic landscape painter, and for geological documentation reasons decided to climb the Austrian Alps to paint a 360-degree panorama. Julia had a chance to tour the museum, and as she looked around, she told me that she realized, "Sometimes, you just have to get out of your own way and accept what's already there."

Your Alter Ego can be a family member who's still living, too. It could be a parent or a grandparent, a sibling or cousin, or an aunt or uncle. When you look into your family history, you may be surprised at who you might find and who inspires you to realize what you're made of and where you come from.

A CEO I met at a conference told me about his experience after graduating from university. He stepped out into the real world and discovered he was ill-prepared for the challenges of professional life, especially the office politics, the harshness of colleagues, and the anxiety of pitching products to customers who didn't want to hear from him. "As someone that isn't a type-A personality, I felt like I was going to live forty years in purgatory if I didn't change something. It was eating me up inside."

He went on to tell me about one of his professors who had this dynamic, playful, and passionate approach to his work. "Professor Martinez seemed fearless and free, and I took every class I could from him. He was my 'arm's-length mentor.' He didn't know it, but I revered him and watched everything he did. So I decided I would embody 'the Professor' and bring him into my work."

What surprised the CEO the most through the process was how much more he felt like himself the more he played with the Alter Ego. "I realized I was more than who I was. I always thought of myself as someone that sat back and let others take the lead because it was for 'those type of people.' The strong-willed, the loud, the extroverts. But I found out that I loved being dynamic, I loved being playful and passionate. It felt like I found this alternate universe inside myself. It was freeing."

Just like the CEO, you may have had a teacher, coach, or mentor you admired and looked up to. Those relationships can be a great place to draw from, too.

PICKING THE BEST

People often ask what or who makes the best Alter Ego. Is it a superhero? Is it a movie or television star? Is it a fictional character? And the answer is always the same:

The best Alter Ego is the one you have the deepest emotional connection with; emotional connection trumps everything.

If there's a character that you've loved since you were fifteen years old then it's worth looking into. If there's an actor you've always admired, start there. If there's a mentor, or a family member like a parent, grandparent, aunt, or uncle, go with it.

The great benefit of the sources we've just run through is because you had so much contact with them, whether by reading, watching, or interacting with them, you can easily adopt and create the same traits and qualities into your Alter Ego or Secret Identity. It's like an "Alter Ego in a Box," because the author, movie director, family history, or daily interactions have already created a strong narrative in your mind.

CREATE YOUR OWN

The final Alter Ego you can choose is one that's already meaningful to you, and you build creatively. This was like my high school and college football days when I merged two of my favorite players. Creating your own takes more mental gymnastics and imagination, but it can also result in a much richer and deeper emotional connection. I jammed

Walter Payton, Ronnie Lott, and a tribe of Native American heroes together to create "Geronimo." I simply cherry-picked the different attributes and qualities from each person and crafted my Secret Identity to take onto the field. And for the skinny kid playing on a field with beasts double my size, it worked.

Another example is Ted, who lost his confidence after suffering a few setbacks in his business and built his Alter Ego in a similar way. Ted owns a business that creates custom technology solutions for clients in the software space to reduce the time to market and the overall cost of their products.

He grew up playing outdoors and doing chores on his family's farm in Honduras. He immigrated to the United States on a scholarship to the University of Vermont, where he graduated with a degree in electrical and computer engineering.

After suffering some setbacks and beginning to lose faith and confidence in himself, he decided to leave this "struggling self" on the sidelines and step into an Alter Ego. When Ted was faced with new business opportunities, making sales calls and pitches, he called upon "Catracho Spearo." *Catracho* is a nickname for Hondurans, and *spearo* is the word for a spearfishing guide in Honduras.

Ted used to go spearfishing all the time and still does occasionally. And when he's seeking new business opportunities, he imagines being in the sixty-foot-deep water, with thirteen-foot great white sharks circling the waters around him as they often would. Every morning, Catracho Spearo goes out in his boat and swims around the waters, full of courage, confidence, and fearlessness, searching for new business opportunities as if he were looking to catch a fish for the day. "Catracho Spearo is focused, mighty, and tough," says Ted.

As he explains, when you're out in the ocean diving for fish, you have minimal resources, and just one breath at a time to dive under, to quickly harness the opportunity for a score. You're looking to spear a bluefin tuna, a halibut, or a large lobster, but you're not the only one seeking prey out there. Big great white sharks scour the depths of the waters beside you, threatening to take not only your opportunity away from you, but also your entire business.

The goal, each day, is to capture an opportunity and carry it safely to your boat.

"I struggled to get through my fear and my weaknesses," says Ted, "but I become Catracho Spearo when I give presentations, when I attend meet-ups, or when I feel uncomfortable with a new project or task. Catracho Spearo says, 'I've been in worse situations before. I just need to load my gun, dive, and take the opportunity when I see it. As long as I step out onto the Field of Play, something will stick, and it's going to stick big-time.'"

What makes Catracho Spearo a strong Alter Ego is that, first, Ted is already passionate about the outdoors and spearfishing, so *bam*! Immediately he's connected to the traits and abilities it takes to succeed in those environments, and he has a deep connection to them. Then he's added the connection to his homeland, Honduras, with the nickname Catracho, which has a deeply meaningful emotional connection to him—it's where he's from, his family still lives there, and he's a proud Honduran. *Bam!* Another deep emotional connection and reverence to honor and use to bring pride to his family of origin and tribe.

Like I said earlier in this chapter, there are multiple ways to find your Alter Ego. Throughout this chapter, I was prompting you with trying to build your Alter Ego by identifying the traits and abilities you'd most want to display on your Field of Play to help you create an Extraordinary World.

Here are some additional questions you can use to uncover those traits:

What are the qualities you admire about other people on your
    Field of Play?
The people exceptional on your Field of Play have what qualities?

If you were prolific at what you do:

How would you think about yourself?
What attitudes would you have about business? Your skills in
    business?
What beliefs would you have?
How would you carry yourself physically?

If it were one year from today, and your identity had been completely altered because of your commitment to your Alter Ego, what
would your most supportive best friends say are the top three things
they are astounded with in regard to your transformation? What
would they be constantly telling other people about your transformation and new results?

When you look back at what you wrote in the Ordinary World
section, what are the opposites of all those weaknesses or perceived
negative attributes you listed?

What are the traits, abilities, attitudes, beliefs, values, and behaviors you'd possess to defeat the Enemy trying to stop you?

Go through the following list of character traits and circle or note
which ones you already possess. Then go through and underline or note
five to ten traits your new Alter Ego or identity is going to possess, as well.

Adaptable	Badass
Adventurous	Brave
Affable	Bright
Affectionate	Broad-Minded
Agreeable	Calculating
Ambitious	Calm
Amiable	Careful
Amicable	Charming
Amusing	Collected

Communicative
Compassionate
Competitive
Complete
Confident
Conscientious
Considerate
Consistent
Controlled
Cool
Courageous
Courteous
Creative
Deadly
Decisive
Determined
Diligent
Diplomatic
Disciplined
Discreet
Dynamic
Easygoing
Emotional
Energetic
Enthusiastic
Extroverted
Exuberant
Fair-Minded
Faithful
Fearless
Fierce

Fiery
Flamboyant
Flexible
Fluid
Forceful
Frank
Friendly
Funny
Generous
Gentle
Giant
Gifted
Good
Gregarious
Hardworking
Helpful
Honest
Humorous
Imaginative
Impartial
Independent
Intellectual
Intelligent
Intuitive
Inventive
Kind
Light
Loved
Loving
Loyal
Mighty

Modest	Sensible
Mysterious	Shadowy
Neat	Sincere
Nice	Slippery
Optimistic	Sociable
Organized	Spirited
Passionate	Straight
Patient	Strong
Persistent	Swift
Pesky	Sympathetic
Pioneering	Systematic
Philosophical	Thoughtful
Placid	Tall
Plucky	Tidy
Polished	Tight
Polite	Tough
Powerful	Tricky
Practical	Unassuming
Proactive	Understanding
Quick-Witted	Velvety
Quiet	Versatile
Rational	Vicious
Reliable	Warmhearted
Reserved	Willing
Resourceful	Witty

After you've selected five to ten character traits that would define your Alter Ego or new identity, how would you exhibit or demonstrate those qualities?

For example, if you chose "powerful," how would you show up in business as "powerful"?

What does that look like to someone else?

What does that feel like to you?

What would you sound like to other people?

What are the attitudes you have about yourself/business that would cause you to be more powerful?

Do you have an example of someone you already perceive to be powerful? How do they act/speak/think?

Use any or all of these questions to bring out the core qualities of your Alter Ego. Another way to go through the exercise and a powerful mindset shift would be to answer those questions as your Alter Ego. If you chose Superman, Wonder Woman, Indiana Jones, Oprah Winfrey, your grandma, Muhammad Ali, Winnie-the-Pooh, Mr. Rogers, Dora the Explorer, Abraham Lincoln, Ellen De-Generes . . . I could go on. Answering the questions as your Alter Ego can release a new level of creativity, awareness, and imagination to what's possible.

As I've said throughout this book, there aren't many rules to this; finding your Secret Identity is a personal process. Use the one right for you. Remember the all-time great athlete Bo Jackson and the story I shared at the very beginning of this book? His Alter Ego was Jason from the Friday the 13th horror movie series. To the average person that sounds completely insane, except his Alter Ego isn't based on what *others* think; it's the meaning *he* pulled from the character, who was unemotional and relentless, the two things Jackson needed to battle his internal enemy of uncontrollable anger.

Thinking through those questions and sinking your proverbial teeth into them will grow your ability to make a tremendous impact on your Extraordinary World. Make it happen!

NAMING YOUR ALTER EGO

For some people, their Alter Ego's name is obvious. If you've chosen a fictional character or someone from real life, then you're going to use that person's name most likely.

If you chose an animal, or if you went into the lab to carefully construct your own Alter Ego after being inspired by the Superpowers of a few, then you're going to need to give it a name.

Why? For the very reason we name the Enemy. Names give shape and form to something. We walk around with names, right? We don't shout, "Hey, man, come here!" or "Hey, guy with no hair on his head and a tattoo on his right forearm!" A name encompasses all the Superpowers and traits and gives your Alter Ego a real identity.

You can pick something like Ted did with Catracho Spearo, or you can create one like Alonto did. You might recall Alonto from page 110 and his Alter Ego, "Big Wave." Alonto and his wife run a marketing company. Born in the Philippines, Alonto immigrated to the United States when he was twelve and went into officer candidate school in the military, going on to serve in the U.S. Navy for eight years before working as an aerospace engineer.

Before starting his business, Alonto had never given a public speech, never gave public presentations, and never billed himself as a speaker. But now he was being asked to speak before live audiences with as many as seven hundred people in attendance.

Alonto's Alter Ego, Big Wave, lives at the side of the stage waiting to be called forth.

Big Wave is one of my favorite Alter Ego names for a few reasons. First, Alonto is a Pacific Islander from the Philippines, and, in his words, he's always "gravitated towards the island explorer lifestyle." Emotional resonance? Check.

Big Wave is inspired by the Rock's character Maui, a demigod who helps the heroine, Moana, in the Disney movie *Moana*. "That's my persona, when it comes to the Alter Ego," Alonto explains. "A lot of it's heritage, a lot of it's the island background, but there's just something about that character that resonates in me. It's someone that fires me up when it comes to thinking about my Alter Ego." Emotional resonance, again? Check, check.

Big Wave is a unique Alter Ego name for a few reasons. One, Alonto has a strong emotional connection to the sea and the island lifestyle. Two, the name holds a cultural significance for Alonto, and it's tied to his family and where he was born and raised. Three, as we talked about earlier, the Alter Ego helps us reach the flow state. Big Wave and flow go exceptionally well together. It's a cool play on words and creates an image connected to flow, so it's like another trigger for Alonto's mind that says it wants to get into the flow state.

Megastar Beyoncé Knowles used the name Sasha Fierce to step into her Alter Ego onstage. As a young girl growing up in a religious family and singing gospel in the choir at church every Sunday, she started out performing in a conservative and modest environment. Last time I checked, there weren't a lot of short skirts and provocative movements at the front of a church. So when she started her pop singing career and was asked to perform dance routines and sing provocative lyrics, it only made sense that it would compete with her existing identity. Creating an Alter Ego to more freely express her creative impulses was a natural part of the process. And I love her use of the name *Fierce*. It has attitude, which I'm sure she needed in the beginning to express this new identity and be intentional about who was going to show up on that Field of Play. And it's pretty hard to argue with her success.

Superstar basketball player Kobe Bryant chose "Black Mamba" as his Alter Ego on the court. Why? In an interview with the *New Yorker*, Kobe says that he got the idea for the nickname from Quentin Tarantino's film *Kill Bill*, in which the snake, known for its agility and aggressiveness, was used as a code name for a deadly assassin.

"I read up on the animal and said, 'Wow, this is pretty awesome,'" Bryant recalled. "This is a perfect description of how I would want my game to be."

The inspiration for your Alter Ego's name can come in many forms, but here's what I know. It typically evolves over time. So don't concern yourself with getting it perfect. Just like when you named your pet for the first time, their name probably evolved over time into a nickname.

When you're choosing your Alter Ego's name, keep in mind that you'll want to have an emotional connection to it (just like Alonto, Kobe, Joanna, Beyoncé, and me).

It should also connect to the Superpowers you'll need to perform on your Field of Play and will act as another trigger reminding you of what you want to tap into during those Moments of Impact.

Here are a few ideas to help kick-start your imagination:

a.   If you've decided to combine two or more sources of inspiration, you could combine their names, like "Black Wonder," a combination of Black Panther and Wonder Woman.
   i.   Buddha-Man (combination of the Buddha and Superman)
   ii.   Napoleon Patton (Napoleon Bonaparte and General George S. Patton)
   iii. Mess-Aldo (Lionel Messi and Cristiano Ronaldo)
   iv.   Grandma Bear (your grandma and a bear)
   v.   Sonic Bond (Sonic the Hedgehog and James Bond)

b.   Give your Alter Ego a title like king, lord, queen, general, commander, princess, master, wizard, champion, expert, etc. And then you could possibly add in your name or add in the name of your Field of Play or the main characteristic you'd like to display or the activity/item you're trying to master:

i.   Commander of the Court ["Insert Title" of the Field of Play]

ii. Joanna, Queen of the Boardroom ["Insert Name," "Insert Title" of the Field of Play]

iii. Matthew, Lord of the Strings ["Insert Name," "Insert Title" of the "Insert Activity/Item You're Trying to Master"]

iv. Susan, Queen of the Close ["Insert Name," "Insert Title" of the "Insert Activity/Item You're Trying to Master"]

v.   Taylor the Unstoppable ["Insert Name" the "Insert Characteristic"]

c. Simply give your Alter Ego the name of the animal or object you may have chosen and add in your name:

i.   The Black Mamba, or Kobe "the Black Mamba" Bryant

ii. The Lion, or, Kerri "the Lion" Herman

iii. The Great White, or Keith "the Great White" Krance

iv. The Rock, or Dwayne "the Rock" Johnson

d. Create a fictional name as a Secret Identity and then add in an adjective that would describe how you'd like to approach your Field of Play, like Beyoncé did with Sasha Fierce:

i.   Tracy Tough

ii. Jackie Calm

iii. Michael Sharp

iv. Kenny Courage

v.   Witty Wynona

e. Take a superhero or character you're inspired by and add it in front of or behind your own name or the profession/role you're in, like Tasmanian Zach:

i.   Editor Bond [Profession + James Bond]

    ii.   Michelle Lennon [Own name + John Lennon]

   iii.   Incredible Baller [Incredible Hulk + Role (basketball player)]

   iv.   Sally Winfrey [Own name + Oprah Winfrey]

    v.   Winston Marshall [Winston Churchill + Own name]

There aren't any rules to this, so just pick a name and start running with it.

This part of the Alter Ego Effect is one of my absolute favorites in the process because it gets your imagination going and empowers *you* to create *your* Extraordinary World. It's also the point where you're in the lab creating the Secret Identity to battle the forces of the Enemy trying to pull you into the Ordinary World. Now we're going to begin the process of adding even more depth, strength, and potency to your Secret Identity by building an Origin Story. Let's get started . . .

CHAPTER 12

BREATHING LIFE INTO
YOUR ALTER EGO

Adolescence is tough.

Beyond the fact that hormones are raging and that trying to tame emotions is like stopping a crash of rhinos, seeing other kids grow faster than you is hard. Especially when you're an athlete trying to compete for starting roles.

Connecticut is a baseball-crazy state. It's a part of the tri-state area that centers on New York City, where millions of people live and commute to. Most of the time you'll find Yankees fans in the area, with the token Mets fans and, even more rare, Red Sox fans. (Okay, there are lots of Mets fans. They just don't admit it.) Tim was no different. He lived and breathed the Yankees.

He was a rare kid, an eleven-year-old with a ton of maturity and leadership skills he could bottle, sell, and make a fortune with. I liked Tim because he was small, gritty, and never quit.

For the past decade, I've taken a handful of young athletes under my wing and mentored them for free. They apply, write an essay, and take an assessment to jump through the hoops to show me who's serious enough to put in the effort. Tim was one of them, and we worked together for years.

For the first couple of years, he made it easy for me. He did his work, built his routines, and started to build a strong mental game foundation. But cracks eventually began to show up. During one of our regular Skype calls he wasn't his usual upbeat, positive self. At first he just chalked it up to having a tough time at the plate. "I'm just not making good contact," he'd say.

We'd work on visualization and imagery techniques, but they weren't helping.

Finally, one day he came back from a tournament in Georgia, where he had a weak performance. He threw out an offhanded comment: "Man, you should've seen how big the guys were down there! They looked like men! I couldn't hit them."

Now, for most people that may just come across as an observation and a teenage thing to say when everyone is racing through puberty at different speeds. But it was the way he said, "I couldn't hit them."

"What do you mean?" I said.

"These guys are getting bigger and bigger. Sometimes I'd go up to the plate, and I'd barely make it up to their chest. Half the guys are growing beards!"

"Tim, is that what you're thinking when you're walking up to the plate?"

"A lot of the time. Unless someone is pitching that's smaller like me. Then I'm fine. But Dad has even started to notice it's getting in my head, and yells from the bleachers all the time to 'just focus on your swing!' He never used to do it, but now that I'm in a slump, he coaches more, and all it does is make me overthink everything."

"Is that how you see yourself now, Tim? Smaller and weaker than the other players, just because they're taller or weigh more?"

He stuttered and stammered, not wanting to admit it, until he finally said, "Well, it's hard not to."

Tim had gone from this superconfident ballplayer to forgetting that the game was about more than just how big you were. There was skill, technique, and strategy, but once he lost his confidence, he lost his skills.

Instead of trying to get Tim to believe in himself again and stop focusing on the size of all the other players, it was a perfect opportunity to create a new version of himself. An Alter Ego that would be a giant.

"Tim. Have you ever heard of Paul Bunyan?"

"No, I don't think so."

"Okay. I want you to find out about him and then call me tomorrow after school," I said.

He was a little confused because I wasn't helping him solve his problem like we'd usually do. "Uhmmm, so we're done?"

"Yep. Talk to you tomorrow."

The next day he called at four o'clock sharp and filled me in on "the great Paul Bunyan."

He went on to tell me Bunyan came from old North American folktales and was a ninety-four-foot-tall lumberjack who helped out the settlers in early America. "He was superstrong, superfast, and really good at swinging his ax," Tim said.

He also said he found some research that said his last name originated from "bon yenne" in Canadian French, which means surprise and astonishment. "He's basically a really good, *really* big guy that knows how to make things happen."

"Awesome," I said. "Remember when we talked about Alter Egos in the past?"

"Yes."

"Well, what if you walked up to the plate as Paul Bunyan? What would Paul Bunyan think about the pitcher on the mound? Would Paul Bunyan be worried about any of the same things you are? He has an ax that can knock down a massive tree with one swing; do you think he could smack a ball out of a ballpark?"

The great thing about working with youngsters is that they're not many years removed from the days when they played make-believe. They let their imaginations run wild with ideas. I could see Tim shift his body language on my computer screen and begin to look more like his old self.

We went back and forth talking more and more about how he could use Paul Bunyan, and leave "small Tim" on the sidelines. "So I can just let Paul take over?" he asked.

"Why not? You've already let someone else take over your swing and your mindset. So why not try someone else?" I responded.

He was game for it.

Just as we looked at all the ways you're currently showing up in your Ordinary World—the behaviors, thoughts, emotions, and traits—you want to identify how your Alter Ego will show up in your Extraordinary World. There are many ways we can make this happen. If you already have an Alter Ego or Secret Identity in mind, then use the layers in this chapter to refine and complete its Identity. If you don't have an Alter Ego yet, no problem; you'll be able to create your Alter Ego from the ground up and then in the following chapters possibly find a source of inspiration that also has those qualities. Or not. There aren't any rules to this. You could create a completely new and unique Alter Ego without any inspiration from the sources we've already listed.

I spoke to a lady once who wanted to be a "good cook" very badly but didn't feel like "it was her thing." "I love the creativity of it, but I think you either have it or you don't." Without getting into a therapy session with her, because I could sense her hesitance came from someone telling her she was terrible, plus I'm completely unqualified to do therapy, I suggested she start taking famous chef Julia Child into the kitchen and see what happens. She'd already told me she loved her. "So why not use her?" I asked.

She thought for a moment and dismissed it as a fun idea, but thought it "probably wasn't for her." That isn't quite the end of the story, but I'll come back to it later.

In the previous chapter, we started to skim the surface of uncovering your Alter Ego and defining its Superpowers. In this chapter, we're going to dig a little deeper and add more depth to it. The more vivid you can make it, the better the chance you'll show up on the Field of Play and win.

When I was struggling and just starting out in my business and began to use "Richard" as my Alter Ego, I didn't have to pause and think about how I wanted to behave. I didn't think about what Richard's thoughts, emotions, beliefs, and values were. I didn't have to think about being worried and fearful as Todd. I knew how Richard would show up because of the inspirations I was pulling from.

If you already have an idea of someone or something you'd like to embody as your Alter Ego, then you can do one of two things with the following exercises. One, answer the questions as you'd see the Alter Ego showing up on the Field of Play. This is called the "Observer Technique." You're simply watching or imagining what they would do, say, think, or feel. The second option is to go through the exercises as if *you are* the Alter Ego. This is the "Immersion Technique." You're thinking through the questions *as* your Alter Ego. This is a great training ground for getting you to play with your Alter Ego.

Something else that has helped a lot of other people with this process, just like Tim, is to read interviews your Alter Ego has given and to watch videos of your Alter Ego to observe their behaviors and mannerisms. If it's a fictional character from books, you'll want to read the books. If it's an animal, find out more about the animal and its hero qualities.

For example, if you chose Oprah, immerse yourself in her world. Details are when the imagination comes alive.

So to help you get started, let's start working through the layers of the Alter Ego Effect model.

LAYER 1: HOW YOU SHOW UP
(Skills, Knowledge, Behaviors, Actions, Reactions)

What abilities, knowledge, behaviors, actions, or reactions do you want your Alter Ego to possess? This could be your ability to control a room with your presence, or the ability to articulate a point in a succinct and charismatic way.

One of my clients was resistant to learning about finances. But when you're running a million-dollar business, that's a severe handicap. After all, business is a game that's kept score with numbers. So instead of developing the skill, he never wanted to look at what was coming in and what was going out or his cash flow.

He could have other people manage and handle his business's money, for sure, but as an owner or executive, if you push the financial reality off entirely, it limits your abilities to win big. Win big with negotiations. Win big with your profits. And win big with you understanding your path to growth. At some point, you'll get taken advantage of. You'll enter a bad deal, or you'll negotiate poor terms. My client had a strong presence in his field, but his business was on life support.

We didn't tear apart why he didn't like numbers, which I knew stemmed from some deep-rooted belief in his relationship with money. He had come from a family that didn't have much. So instead we set up Financial Fridays, the day that finances would get taken care of, including all financial meetings. And instead of him showing up for those meetings, his Alter Ego, who loved finances and was diligent with the details and numbers, showed up.

When we walked through your Ordinary World, we looked at some of your current actions and behaviors, and the results you've been getting on your Field of Play. Now we want to look at how your Alter Ego will perform on the Field of Play, in that Moment of Impact.

What are your actions and behaviors? For example, in negotiations, leaning forward may indicate an aggressive stance, while leaning back can signal indifference. If you're talking clearly and calmly, then that can signal you're confident and in control. Is one behavior or personality trait better than the other? Not really. It just depends on your intent.

What matters is how you want your Alter Ego to show up. If you want your Alter Ego to talk quietly and calmly and with an air of authority, then that's how you'll want your Alter Ego to show up. If you want your Alter Ego to have the Superpower of excitement and liveliness and eagerness, then that's how they'll show up. Of course, this can be primarily influenced by the source or inspiration for your Alter Ego. Elon Musk would behave differently in a job interview than Abraham Lincoln, Ellen DeGeneres, Simon Cowell, Barack Obama, or Oprah.

What are the behaviors that your Alter Ego embodies? How will it act? Will its posture change? Will it hold its head differently? Will your facial expressions change? I have an athlete in the NBA who has a slight squint in his eyes when he's facing off with an opponent. It's there to shut his mouth, so he doesn't talk trash. He stares at them for long stretches of time, until they break the gaze. He wants to make them uncomfortable.

Think about the physical mannerisms your Alter Ego may have. (This isn't a must, but some people use them as a way to anchor into their Alter Ego.) A physical mannerism can be a manifestation of a positive attribute. For example, Cary Grant had a certain way he held his whiskey glass that made him feel more refined. If "refined" was the attribute he wanted, then this was his way of acting that way. If someone says something to you in a meeting, and you typically shoot from the hip and fire a response only to regret it later, will your Alter Ego simply pause and calmly respond with a "Let me think about it" or "That's interesting" or "Let me check my calendar and get back to you"? If someone asks a question during a meeting and you never raise your hand, will your Alter Ego lean in and speak up instead?

If you need to, think back on the old actions you were taking during your Moments of Impact in your Ordinary World, then think about the new action you want your Alter Ego to take. Or, if you already know who or what you'll be borrowing your Alter Ego from, what do some of their mannerisms look like?

You can also consider other physical qualities, such as what would your Alter Ego look like? When I asked an entrepreneur what other successful entrepreneurs looked like, he told me they're well dressed with a tailored look. That's not the image I picture, and I know quite a few successful entrepreneurs who dress in jeans or shorts and T-shirts. But my opinion holds zero weight. My client was creating his world, and in his world, entrepreneurs dress in style.

In your world, how does your Alter Ego dress? Is there a specific article of clothing, like a hat or scarf it wears? Is there a style of dress you quickly associate with your Alter Ego? Years ago, I was flipping through a magazine while sitting at an airport terminal, and I saw a picture of four men in tuxedos. One man caught my eye. His suit jacket's sleeves were hemmed about two inches shorter than the other men's, and it was striking how much he stood out. I liked it, so I adopted it, too. Who was the man? Frank Sinatra. When I looked at Sinatra in his suit, I saw confidence and style.

Think about your Alter Ego's presence. How do they carry themselves in a room? Mark Cuban, outspoken entrepreneur, owner of the Dallas Mavericks basketball team, and one of the stars of the television show *Shark Tank*, tends to sit back in his chair on the show in a very relaxed pose. Sometimes he'll lean forward when he's interested in someone's idea. Daniel Craig, when he plays James Bond, has a pronounced swagger with his shoulders when he walks.

Here's a helpful list of possible attributes you could tap into:

Adaptable	Affectionate
Adventurous	Alert

Ambitious

Analytical

Appreciative

Bold

Calm

Cautious

Centered

Charming

Confident

Cooperative

Courageous

Courteous

Creative

Curious

Decisive

Diplomatic

Disciplined

Discreet

Easygoing

Efficient

Empathetic

Enthusiastic

Extroverted

Flamboyant

Flirtatious

Focused

Friendly

Funny

Generous

Gentle

Happy

Honest

Honorable

Hospitable

Humble

Idealistic

Imaginative

Independent

Industrious

Innocent

Inspirational

Intelligent

Introverted

Just

Kind

Loyal

Mature

Merciful

Meticulous

Natural

Focused

Nurturing

Obedient

Objective

Observant

Optimistic

Organized

Passionate

Patient

Patriotic

Pensive

Perceptive

Persistent

Persuasive

Philosophical	Spiritual
Playful	Spontaneous
Private	Spunky
Proactive	Studious
Professional	Supportive
Proper	Talented
Protective	Thrifty
Quirky	Tolerant
Resourceful	Traditional
Responsible	Trusting
Sensible	Uninhibited
Sensual	Unselfish
Sentimental	Whimsical
Simple	Wholesome
Socially Aware	Wise
Sophisticated	Witty

LAYER 2: WHO YOU ARE
(Attitudes, Beliefs, Values, Perceptions, Expectations)

At this level, you want to dig into that space where attitudes, beliefs, values, perceptions, and expectations rest.

"My Alter Ego believes . . ." Fill in the blank.

"My Alter Ego believes he's an engaging writer who draws people into all his stories, and readers are excited about everything he creates."

"My Alter Ego believes she's a powerful presenter on the stage. Her mere presence captivates and moves an audience."

Now, what about changing up the word *believes* with *knows*? Reread those sentences with this simple substitution.

"My Alter Ego knows she's a powerful presenter on the stage. Her mere presence captivates and moves an audience."

There's a big difference between "knowing" and "believing"; I want you to *know* you're great.

Brian works for a massive insurance company, and while he had great ideas, he never spoke up. He classified himself an introvert and often felt intimated by type-A people in board meetings, which was more a result of a bullying older brother. His Alter Ego, however, was Mister Fantastic, from *The Fantastic Four*. His Alter Ego wasn't just about changing his behaviors, it was about changing the thoughts. "I've got brilliant ideas to share and everyone wants to hear them." Brian's Alter Ego, the brilliant scientist Reed Richards, would never have the thought that he shouldn't share his ideas.

What does your Alter Ego believe about themselves? Or know about themselves? What do they believe about the Field of Play they're standing on?

As you're thinking about your Alter Ego, think about what it would believe about itself, and then about the world, which might include other people. If you're in a meeting with possible clients or trying to close a sale, what would they be thinking about the Alter Ego? "They can't wait for the chance to work with me," your Alter Ego would believe. "The audience absolutely wants to hear me speak," your Alter Ego would think right before it went onstage.

Sitting in a room with Oprah, you'd be thinking different things about her than you would about a lion or Lincoln or Malala.

You can also consider your Alter Ego's values. There are hundreds of values that may or may not serve you on your Field of Play. Fairness, justice, wealth, joy, family, friendships, loyalty, and power are examples of values that may help or hinder your Alter Ego depending on how you need it to show up during your Moment of Impact.

This is a judgment-free zone. There are no good or bad values—just values that help you perform and those that hold you back. Power is a value—sometimes it's healthy, and other times, valuing too much of it leaves you alone and isolated.

You can also consider what thoughts your Alter Ego will have. If you aren't sure, try this: What thoughts will your Alter Ego never have? If you read through the Ordinary World chapters and you realized you currently show up thinking, I can't pitch investors and get them to close, then your Alter Ego is going to think, I pitch investors, and get them to agree to our deals all the time.

Once again, remember, all of these questions, layers, and examples aren't 100 percent prerequisites to using the Alter Ego Effect and benefiting from it. Most likely you've already used something similar at some point in your life. Now I'm just handing you the keys to a more robust system. Just as many streets and avenues lead to the center of town, there are many ways to help you connect to this concept, use it, and lead your Heroic Self onto the Field of Play.

THE PACKAGE

One evening about six weeks after the conversation with the aspiring cook who wanted to find her inner Julia Child, I came home to a package waiting for me. I didn't recognize the name on the package, but I opened it to see what was inside. After I peeled open the cardboard box, I discovered a beautifully wrapped gift box with a note card attached.

I pulled the note off the ribbon it was clinging to and it read, "You were right.—Julia."

The box was filled with some of the absolute best chocolate brownies I've ever had. And I only wish I'd gotten the idea earlier to tell people to tap into their inner Julia Child.

MORE EXERCISES TO BUILD YOUR ALTER EGO

These exercises are a collection of some I've used with clients in the past to help them get greater clarity with their Alter Ego. Try one, try them all, possibly something else will click for you.

Exercise 1: Relax yourself and imagine watching your character growing up from birth until now. What shaped them? What do they do differently from you? How do they look? How do they speak? What words or phrases do they use? What feelings do they have? What skills and capabilities do they possess?

Exercise 2: Imagine yourself in a lab creating this Alter Ego. What are you adding, what are you taking away? One of my clients did this exercise by imagining it was his twin brother, and they were separated at birth. His brother was stuck in a black hole of wisdom and learned all the highest-level skills of his sport. My client tapped into his Alter Ego when he wanted to show up on the playing field as a source of infinite wisdom.

Exercise 3: Write out a full conversation between you and the Alter Ego. I had one client pretend she was stuck in an elevator with her Alter Ego, and they had no one else to talk to but each other. I had her imagine asking her Alter Ego how her mind worked before a competition. What do they think of competitors, or is the Alter Ego so confident that they don't even care or think about the competitors? Did the Alter Ego worry about anything? What were they striving for? She observed the Alter Ego; what did she look like? How did she hold herself? How did she move? What expressions did she have? Then I asked her how she would describe the Alter Ego to a friend after they escaped from the elevator?

In a speech given to the Stanford Graduate School of Business in 2014, Oprah Winfrey was inspiring graduates to find purpose and meaning in their work. She encouraged them to find allies to help them in hard times as her best friend, Gayle King; Stedman Graham; and others have done for her. But she also said something quite profound when discussing the source of her power: "I come as one, I stand as ten thousand. When I walk into a room . . . I will literally sit and call on that ten thousand." She was paraphrasing "Our Grandmothers," a poem from Maya Angelou. And the source of that power she was explaining, you'll find in the next chapter.

CHAPTER 13

THE HEROIC ORIGIN STORY

Imagine you are sitting at an outside cafe sipping on a cappuccino, tea, or whatever your taste buds were craving, and you see a frantic old man running down the street chasing a purple balloon. What would you be thinking?

Look at that crazy old man.

Now imagine this . . .

You sit down with your drink of choice at the same cafe, and an elderly man sits at the table next to you. He has a purple balloon. You strike up a conversation with him and ask about the balloon he has tied to his wrist, and he begins to tell you the story of his life. He starts by telling you about this spirited and adventurous girl he met while he was a young boy. They immediately bonded over their lively imaginations. The girl had this abandoned house she'd turned into her playhouse, where they spent hours and days hatching schemes and playing make-believe.

They grew up, they married, and they fixed up the old abandoned house and turned it into their home. They never had children, and they never saved enough to travel the world like they thought. Through it all, they still dreamed of visiting this magical place someday. Each week they'd save every penny they had for the trip, but something—life and its responsibilities and its bills and needs—always got in their way. With each circumstance, they'd break open their "travel savings jar," empty it, and start again. Years passed by, and he talked about how the two grew old together as best friends. He continues to tell you how he *finally* planned their magical trip to surprise her, so they could take their "great adventure."

By this time you're leaning in, engaged in this man's story, and you can't wait for his wife to walk out with her tea, so you can meet her.

Except he tells you his wife passed away, leaving the old man alone in their big old house. (Cue the tear-jerking and lump in your throat.)

He's now decided to attach as many balloons as possible to his home, to lift it off the ground and float it all the way down to their magical place. There he'll be able to fulfill their lifetime dream and show her he finally made it. And the purple balloon he's holding is the final balloon to achieve his dream and set sail on his adventure.

Now, if that purple balloon became untethered from his wrist and he got up to chase after it, what would be your reaction? Wouldn't you think:

There's not a chance in hell I'm going to let that balloon get away from him.

Why?

Because the man and the balloon have emotional context. There's a story attached to them. And now it's attached to you, too.

If you haven't already figured it out, this is the opening scene to the movie *Up*, by Pixar Entertainment. And the two lovebirds were Carl and Ellie hoping to get to their dream destination, Paradise Falls. It's one of my all-time favorite movies.

Every hero has an Origin Story. It's the story of how they became who they are today, how their Superpowers were bestowed upon them, and what drives them internally to defeat their Enemies—the ones in the external world and the ones inside them. And the mission they're on to realize their Extraordinary World.

As heart-wrenching as the opening of the movie *Up* is, learning Carl's backstory also sets the stage for the rest of the movie. Now we know why he rigs up his house with thousands of helium balloons to sail away in search of Paradise Falls, finishing the adventure he promised his wife they'd go on together. Learning Carl's story, we now understand what's motivating our curmudgeonly hero, and it draws us in emotionally to his story.

We're hooked. We feel for Carl. Why? Because on some level, we see ourselves in him. We know what it feels like to have the responsibilities of life suck us further away from our dreams. We know what it's like to plan and save for tomorrow, only to find that the tomorrow we dreamed of has disappeared. We know what it's like to have dreams dashed like Carl and Ellie, who never had children and who never took that trip. We know what it's like to have our hearts broken. We know what it's like to feel the tragic sting of despair, only to see a tiny twinkle of light spark a thought that maybe we can turn things around. We cheer for Carl as he musters his courage and gathers his strength and tests his resolve to move the home he built with Ellie to Paradise Falls.

We cheer for our hero because his story strikes a chord in us.

Let's be frank. In our daily lives there's just crap we have to deal with. There are frustrations, annoyances, and unforeseen circumstances we get hit with. The Enemy feeds off this because it's a perfect opportunity to pull you into the Ordinary World, distract you, or make you doubt yourself or hide from your real desires. Your Enemy pushes and pulls and will try to steal away the glory found on your Field of Play.

However, your Alter Ego can be there to pull you back and lay down a potent defense to the Enemy. And your Alter Ego's Origin Story is one of the tools we use.

So, my question for you is, what is the driving force for your Alter Ego? What propels your Alter Ego to stand up to the Enemy and to defeat it at every turn?

The driving force you seek is usually found in your Alter Ego's Origin Story. Just as you've been living out a story, we're going to connect with a new, more dominant story that your Alter Ego will live out.

FIND YOUR ALTER EGO THROUGH STORY

I wasn't in the taxi for more than thirty seconds before I received a text message:

"Hey, Todd. It's Mitch. Great to connect tonight. I'd love to meet with you to see if you could help me make this transition a success."

"Of course. Can you do lunch on Wednesday?"

"Perfect. Let's meet at my office, and we'll order something in."

"Sounds good."

Mitch and I met in 2011, at a small dinner in New York with four other people. A friend and I take turns hosting small gatherings of interesting people. We invite people from finance, tech, arts, entertainment, charity, business, and, of course, sports, to connect people and have great conversation. This dinner happened to be my friend Jayson Gaignard's turn to curate the guests. He's a master at it and even wrote an amazing book on the process.

At the dinner, I sat next to Mitch, a man who had built a successful career on Wall Street. We connected over our love of sports, and he grilled me on high performance and the mental game. I could tell his questions were to help him sort out some of the uncertainty and volatility of his new situation. He had recently transitioned out of a role he'd been in for years and was recruited by a large financial company to lead a new business unit. It was demanding a completely new skill set and leadership ability.

We ended up exchanging cards and promised to connect again soon. The dinner ended late into the night, we said our good-byes to new friends, and I walked to the street corner to hail a taxi. That's when the text exchange happened.

At our lunch, I walked him through an assessment I do with all new clients, and it was clear that an Alter Ego might be the tool I'd use to help him. I explained the concept to him, then I asked him, "Is there anyone that you truly admire and respect for the leadership abilities?"

"That's easy. My bubbe."

I hadn't heard the term before, so I said, "Bubbe?"

"It's the Jewish term for grandma. My grandmother was incredible. And she's the most inspiring person in my life."

Mitch went on to tell me how she grew up in Poland, where she got married and had four children. When World War II broke out, her family was torn apart, her husband and two older boys taken away. Her husband hadn't survived, but by some miracle, after the war ended, she was able to find the two boys who had been separated from her. She ended up bringing them to Canada, then eventually New York City to meet up with other relatives who had immigrated to the United States. Because of the war, she had virtually nothing except eighty-four dollars "and an iron rod for a spine."

She raised her family in a tiny studio apartment in the Lower East Side of Manhattan, "worked her ass off, and showered her kids with love but in a very strict home.

"My dad would tell me stories of the 'old country ladle,' one of the few things that made the trip over from Europe. And how she had it hanging between two tiny windows in their apartment and would threaten them with it if they ever got out of line. 'Nobody wanted that thing to get pulled off the wall,' he'd say."

He continued: "Grandma raised four incredibly successful children. Two are doctors, one is a real estate developer, and my dad became a university professor."

The more he talked about her, the more his entire physiology changed. He beamed, and you could tell he was extremely proud to come from that history. I looked at him and said, "Mitch, we've got your Alter Ego."

I walked him through the entire process we've already been going through, to develop his Alter Ego and then finally choose an "Artifact" to represent his Alter Ego. (I'll explain this in the chapter on Totems and Artifacts.)

When it came to the name for his Alter Ego, he never shared it. He knew exactly what it would be, and he wanted to keep it private. But its core Superpowers were strength, courage, and conviction. And he used her Origin Story and his challenges to create a motivation to drive him forward in his new career.

Throughout any one of the last few chapters, you may have already discovered and connected with your Alter Ego's motivation. Having a story deeply rooted in your mind for why you chose or whom or what you chose helps you Activate this Heroic Self. Some people who thought they'd found their Alter Ego changed it once they found a different Alter Ego in a more resonant and meaningful story. Again, there's no right or wrong here, just what's right for you.

If you're not sure about the identity of your Alter Ego, then think about the stories of real-life people or fictional characters from television or movies or books or comics. Is there a story you're drawn to? Why? What about that story has grabbed you by the heartstrings or captivated you?

If no story comes to mind, try reading about successful people in your chosen space. Biographies and autobiographies are great sources to find someone's story, which may align closely with yours, and *boom*! There's your Alter Ego.

Most of the time, it's the simplest Origin Stories that become the most powerful.

The Origin Story fills in the blanks and explains where your Alter Ego came from. The story explains how it developed its Superpowers, why it needs those Superpowers, and what they fight against.

Without a story, you risk missing the emotional connection to your Alter Ego. Building and using an Alter Ego is more than an intellectual exercise—it is about transforming how you perform and show up during your Moment of Impact. That's the only way you can enter your Extraordinary World. The Origin Story helps you to latch on to the Alter Ego's identity, immerse yourself in it, and act through it.

Remember, this isn't about "pretending." That's why the "fake it till you make it" philosophy has fallen flat for most. This is about embodying it, just as the study of the young children that used Batman or Dora the Explorer had greater results when they truly became them when faced with hard puzzles compared to the children who just pretended.[1]

CORE DRIVERS

In the Field of Play Model, there's a collection of Core Drivers that, when you identify yourself with them, are deeply motivating and "drive you" to think, feel, and act in certain ways. They also come layered with a story because they have narratives attached to them and definitions of what it means to be a part of them.

In chapter 3 I outlined the Core Drivers in the first layer that impact your world. The most common:

Family
Community
Nation
Religion
Race
Gender
Identifiable Group (police officers, soldiers, farmers, tribe)
Idea
Cause

It's anything you connect to that is somehow bigger than you. Some specific Origin Stories tend to have more emotional resonance than others for a reason. There's a driving force behind these stories, very similar to your mission for creating an Alter Ego. For instance, when I'm working with Olympic athletes, many Origin Stories connect to their cultures or nationalities. Some athletes transform their performances knowing they're one of the chosen, selected to represent their country. They're driven to make their country proud. Competing in the Olympics changes the story in some athletes' minds and hearts.

When I'm working with Olympic athletes, I'm always looking to see if I need to dial up, or sometimes dial down, the nationalistic pride. For some people, the story about representing their country causes them to collapse inward. The pressure becomes too great. Sometimes athletes have no care or attachment to their country. Sometimes it's that they want to make their hometown proud, or they want to make their families proud.

I worked with a biathlete from a Nordic country a few years back, and it took a few misfires before we found a driving force he connected to. If you're not familiar with this grueling sport, biathletes strap on a pair of skis no wider then 7 centimeters or 2.8 inches and race around flat, uphill, and downhill terrain carrying a rifle on their back. Then they race into a shooting area, and, within seconds, grab their rifle and fire at a target no bigger than 4.6–11.4 centimeters or 1.8–4.5 inches diameter from a distance of fifty meters! You want something hard, try it. These athletes are impressive!

Back to our biathlete. I thought we'd get him into his flow state by using his country as driving force. I was wrong. The more we talked about his country and experimented with it as a source of motivation, the flatter it fell. It didn't "rev his engine." We had to course correct, which we did—thankfully—by stumbling onto his family's story. He came from a long line of biathletes, and during World War II, many of his family members were used as scouts and spies while traversing the tough Nordic terrain. Some of them died in combat and others were awarded medals for their bravery. He found his Alter Ego's driving force in the Origin Story of his family legacy. It gave my client a tremendous source of pride and meaning to represent his family. And those family members became a tribe of warriors he used as his Alter Ego to dig deep when the races got hard.

That was the heart of his Alter Ego's Origin Story.

HOW TO CREATE YOUR ALTER EGO'S ORIGIN STORY

Aligning with an existing story is one of the easiest paths and the one I usually recommend clients start with. Take your Alter Ego and find their Origin Story.

I'm sure I don't have to say this, but I'll play captain obvious, so there are no misunderstandings: make sure whatever Origin Story you choose is one that you connect to. If Batman is your Alter Ego, and you're using his Origin Story, then you'd better be sure you emotionally connect with his backstory. Maybe, just like Batman, you had something traumatizing happen to you when you were younger and so you resonated with his deep sense of "making it right." Or maybe you connect with his sense of honor and the anonymity of good deeds. Or the fact he wears a suit that represents the exact thing he feared the most.

I had a client once who used Batman to help her transition from a marketing career into a career in theater. She had avoided the thing she most wanted to do her entire life and would never allow herself to pursue, for fear of failing. So just like Batman, she faced the fear and aligned herself with his story to step into an Extraordinary World.

"It was tough at first. Walking away from fourteen years of hard work and a successful career felt crazy. But it was crazier never to answer that question of 'what if?' I went from expensive dinners and drinks with friends to staying home and eating noodle soup. But I thought, I'm just going through the preparation stage like Christian Bale's character in *Batman Begins*. And honestly, I was never happier. But I couldn't have made it happen without my Secret Identity and showing up at auditions with the confidence of Bruce and Batman."

HOW A SINGLE MOM FOUND HER FIRE

Maggie is an entrepreneur and a single mom working hard to raise her two kids in London. She found her Alter Ego through the Origin Story of an inspiring author/celebrity that mirrored her own struggles.

When we started working together, she was terrified of sharing her stuff with the world. She was doing okay, but she wasn't achieving the big bumps in business or making the impact that she wanted. She was taking action, but she was playing it small. Playing small isn't a bad thing if that's your goal and it's enough for you, but it wasn't enough for Maggie. She had a big dream and a big desire to grow her business. She had big ideas for growing her impact and influence, but she wasn't executing or following through on the projects she started.

As she was telling me about her personal story, all I could think was, Her story sounds so similar to J. K. Rowling's—a single mom who could barely rub two pennies together. She wrote her first Harry Potter book in cafes while she and her daughter lived on public assistance.[2] Did she sell her manuscript on its first submission? No way. She heard "no" twelve times before a publisher took a shot on her.[3] And after all her success with Harry Potter, when she wrote the next series under a pen name, it was rejected.[4]

"There's no reason you can't be the next J. K. Rowling," I told Maggie. "She faced rejection before becoming one of the most revered authors. You can create and ship your content, too. Who cares how many times it gets rejected because, in the end, you'll win, you'll persevere, because that's who you are. You're a fighter. You never give up. You're fighting to make a better life for your children, and you have something special to share with the world."

My words were met with quiet sniffles. I knew I had plucked an emotional chord. Just like in the movie *Up*, when we feel a resonant emotion in our hearts, we know it. Maggie felt the light of truth, and she saw herself and her own story in Rowling's.

Maggie chose J. K. Rowling as her Alter Ego and merged her Origin Story with the famous author's, creating a profoundly motivating force to launch her onto her Field of Play, entrepreneurship. Her Alter Ego would say, "I may go through a lot of rejection because that's just what we all do. But I keep going. I won't quit because I have this thing inside of me that's aching to get out, and I'm going to listen to it."

J. K. Rowling's story resonated with Maggie, so Rowling was an easy choice for her Alter Ego. Did she have to choose Rowling? Nope. She could have chosen a different one, say her grandmother, and then attached Rowling's story to it to create the emotional oomph she needed for the Origin Story.

If you're leveraging the Origin Story of anyone or anything, be sure you have the emotional connection to it. Television and movies or books can offer you rich, deep, and meaningful Origin Stories. All you need to do is find the one you connect to and that resonates with you at your core.

Creating a killer Origin Story for your Alter Ego is about knowing what will fuel its ascent. MaryAnn, who co-owns the auto repair shop with her husband, found that her Alter Ego's story is largely driven by her desire to show women that they can succeed in male-dominated environments and industries. Her story began when she and her husband started to join business and trade associations and began attending events. "I would go to these events, and I was, maybe, one of three, often two women in the room out of two hundred and fifty people. I remember thinking at first, Wow, this could feel intimidating."

Never content to remain a wallflower, observing the Field of Play from afar, MaryAnn gathered her courage and started introducing herself to the men and striking up conversations with them. "I had to speak up because the men thought I was just there helping and supporting my husband in his business. They didn't realize we were equal partners."

Recently, MaryAnn pivoted from just the auto repair shop to open a consulting practice to help small business shops grow their business and better serve customers.

"I wanted to be an example to other women," MaryAnn told me, "because I knew that there were women in the industry who needed support and to be validated. I wanted other women to see me up there and out there so they could then see themselves out there and up there, too, and they would realize they had something valuable to offer their industries and communities."

Every Alter Ego has a driving force. Look deep within to find yours. What big mission do you feel your Alter Ego is called to undertake? It may not be serving a large community; it may be smaller, like your family.

It may also be personal. Joanne uses a mix of stories from her life and from the people in her life, like her father and her grandfather, to create something uniquely hers. Joanne came from a very working-class background in Manchester, England. Her father came from a moneyed family, her mom from working-class roots. When her father married her mother, his family disowned him. Thrust out of his own tribe, he was forced to make his way in the world—at times, this meant Joanne and her two brothers grew up quite poor.

"I'm never going to be poor," Joanne says. The "I'm never going to be poor" is the driving force in her Alter Ego's Origin Story, or at least that's what she thought until we discussed it further. She credits her Alter Ego with helping to pull her out of her tribe and giving her the confidence and courage to go create a new one. "I'm the only girl out of all my male cousins. I was the only one who didn't go to a good school. It was deemed that as a girl, you purely were there to clean the house, cook, pour tea . . . you didn't get a good education. So, I went out and got my own education."

When you look at that story, do you think it was really about "never being poor"? I didn't. So I challenged her on it.

I said, "Joanne, everything about what you just told me sounded like it was more about showing the family that abandoned your family that you could make it. Yeah, you didn't want to be poor. But I feel like it was a lot more about honor, honoring your mom and dad and showing the other side of the family they can't put their boot on your dreams."

Through a few tears and a lump in her throat, she shot back, "You're goddamn right it was."

That's the kind of emotion I want you to have.

Your Alter Ego can be "For Something" or "Against Something" or "Both." Joanne was for her family and against the treatment her father and mother received. And it's hard to argue with Joanne's success. She's a tremendous fighter.

ARE YOU INSPIRED BY AN ANIMAL?

Like Julia, you may have chosen an animal as your Alter Ego and may be wondering how you can build out its Origin Story. Focus on the traits the animal represents that pulled you in. What does a turtle represent to you? What does an eagle, a panther, or a python mean to you?

You can look to stories from indigenous peoples, in which animals and nature were symbolic, so there may be cultural stories about an animal. I work with a client from the Cayman Islands, and his Alter Ego is the sea turtle. It's not vicious, but it goes off on adventures into the depths of the sea, and it survives—for a long time. Some sea turtle species live 150 years or more. To my client, the sea turtle is wise, fearless, and respected. In this instance, the Origin Story was rooted in both where he was from and an animal that personified the qualities he wanted on his Field of Play, corporate sales.

He named his Alter Ego Tortuga. In the beginning, he simply tapped into the traits he admired, but over time he created an Origin Story for Tortuga. "It was my way of connecting to this wise, calm, and fearless self and honor it when I was out doing my thing."

If you've chosen an animal as your Alter Ego, try searching for stories and watch documentaries on the animal. The more you know, the more you can tap into its supernatural abilities. Research what experts have written; watch any interviews they've given or speeches they've delivered. Often their passion is infectious. If you've never seen the Irwin family from Australia talk about animals, you're missing out. They can convince you that anything is "truly amazing."

Heck, even children's books can be a great source of characters or animals with empowering, inspiring, and meaningful Origin Stories.

Your Alter Ego's Origin Story doesn't have to be a novel or epic poem. A few short sentences will do, or if words are clumsy for you, that's okay. As long as you can tap into the emotional pull for your Alter Ego, that's all we care about. It's the same idea we discussed earlier; there are many ways to apply the Alter Ego Effect. So, whether you build the Alter Ego to play with a new idea, you build it to tap into a new creative self, or you build it to help get out of your own way and conquer the Hidden Forces that have stopped you in the past, the Origin Story is just another way we help your Alter Ego come to life.

Now that you've built an Alter Ego, named it, and connected to it with the mission and Origin Story, it's time to Activate it.

CHAPTER 14

ACTIVATING YOUR ALTER EGO WITH A TOTEM OR ARTIFACT

In 1940, while the world was being pulled into the second great war in a generation, the British bulldog Winston Churchill was about to be named prime minister of Great Britain. Ever since I was a young kid on our family farm in Canada, I was fascinated with him. There was this incredible mythology about him and a legend that's lived on for decades because of how he led the British people and Europe through a perilous time.

I remember reading in a biography how he would use his hats to evoke a different personality. When he received the telegram that he would be the new prime minister, he was filled with a grave concern he couldn't lead the country during such a difficult time. But as he was getting ready to travel to London to see the king and accept the role, he stood in front of his wall of hats and proclaimed, "Which Self should I be today?"[1]

In the 2017 movie *Darkest Hour*, they actually show the moment he grabs his top hat, utters the phrase, and walks out the door.

Churchill isn't the only one to use what I call a *Totem* to be more intentional about his performance.

Martin Luther King had perfect vision, but he still wore glasses. If you're familiar with this great leader of the civil rights movement, you might be a bit surprised. In some of King's most famous photographs, you can see him wearing eyeglasses, except he wasn't wearing them to see better. He was wearing them because, in his words, "I felt they made me look more distinguished." You can actually find Martin Luther King's glasses on display at Atlanta Hartsfield Airport.

Here you have two large figures from history, Winston Churchill and Martin Luther King, and they both overcame the challenges they faced by leveraging elements of the Alter Ego Effect. They used the power of the human imagination, and both used the power of a Totem to help Activate it, something you'll do in this final stage of making the transformation complete.

THE POWER OF SYMBOLIC MEANING

Imagine you're a doctor with the traditional white coat on and you slide a stethoscope around your neck. What traits do you associate with a doctor? Poise? Respect? Care? Compassion? Intelligence? Dedication?

Now imagine you walk into an auditorium filled with students taking exams. And you find your desk to sit down and take your test. How would you feel as the doctor sitting down to take the exam? What would you say to yourself? What type of emotion would be running through your body? What do you notice about other people as they look at you in your white lab coat ready to take the exam? What story are they telling themselves about how you're going to do on the test?

Well, it turns out, you'd most likely do a lot better on the test.

In a study by the Kellogg School of Management,[2] researchers found that it's not just about what you wear, but also whether you understand what its "symbolic meaning" is. The study looked at the effects of a white coat on students' attention and accuracy. The researchers found that:

- Attention did not increase when the coat was *not* worn or was associated with a painter.
- Attention only increased when the coat was a) worn and b) associated with a doctor.
- The influence of clothes depends on wearing them and their symbolic meaning.

So basically, if you thought the coat was a painter's coat, nothing changed. The moment you put on a doctor's coat, your attention and accuracy improved.

This phenomenon is called "enclothed cognition." Enclothed cognition only happens when you understand the "symbolic meaning" of the item *and* the "psychological experience of wearing the item which constantly reminds you of what the item represents."[3] So in the experiment, the symbolic power of the white coat changed depending on what you were told it represents. The painter or artist's smock makes you more artistic. The doctor's coat makes you more attentive. And the lab coat makes you more careful. (We wouldn't want you blowing up the lab, now, would we?!)

Somewhere, tucked within yourself, you have a story about what doctors represent, how they act, what they think, and how they feel. If I told you just to take the traits you identified—poise, compassion, intelligence—and try to bring them to life, it's going to seem more difficult. You'd have to think about it first. Now, the moment I hand you a "symbol" that represents a doctor, like a stethoscope or a lab coat, you start to "enclothe" yourself in the traits you've associated with them. Now when I tell you to act like a doctor, it's much easier to embody their traits and get similar results to whatever you associate with them.

I hope you see the ramifications of this, and the fun you're about to have. While you've just done a lot of hard work identifying, building, and creating your Alter Ego, now you're going to find a Totem that acts as a symbol to Activate your Alter Ego. Just like Winston Churchill, Bo Jackson, David Bowie, Martin Luther King, myself, and thousands of others.

THE POWER OF SYMBOLS, OBJECTS, AND ENVIRONMENTS

We live in a world filled with symbols, and the human mind has this fantastic capacity to create a sense of meaning from virtually anything. Any object can hold some meaning, whether it's cultural or intensely personal. Your imagination can create vivid stories around seemingly random items. And you can associate emotions, ideas, stories, and the actions of what that item represents.

Because you and I come from different backgrounds, each of these items will mean something different to both of us: A tractor. A baseball. A bald eagle. A police officer's badge. An apron. Your country's flag. A book. A pair of glasses. A cape.

I could go on. Just take something simple like the pair of glasses. MLK attributed being more distinguished to them. I used glasses to be more "confident, articulate, and decisive." A famous NBA client uses glasses to be more "mild-mannered like Clark Kent off the court" and as a "shield from the public to protect his personal life." One object, many meanings, for many purposes.

Have you ever been around someone when they lost something, and they freaked out? To you it seemed like nothing, but to them it meant something. It "symbolized" something. Heck, if you take the average person today and they lose their smartphone, it's like they've been amputated from the rest of the world. We've all seen people become frantic over a lost phone, right?

Well, it's because it represents our relationships, our contacts, our work, and our memories with photos and stored conversations. It represents our security, because what if someone finds it and hacks their way in? It seems there are very few items that carry more meaning than a smartphone today.

When I give speeches on the topics of "Peak Performance" or the "Mental Game of Winning," I talk about the power of symbols. One of my most popular talks featured four mannequins with blankets draped over them. One by one, I would reveal each mannequin to the audience. The first would be wearing a police officer's uniform. I'd turn to the audience and ask, "What does seeing a police officer's uniform mean to you?"

Then, one by one, I revealed each mannequin. One would be dressed in an army uniform, one as a doctor, and the last one as Superman or Wonder Woman.

After each reveal, I'd turn to the audience and ask them what each uniform meant. "Shout out your answers in one or two words," I'd instruct. I was met with a hodgepodge of responses. The uniforms symbolized something different to everyone, but oftentimes there would be a consistent theme. As I explained, there were no right or wrong answers. The only right answer was the one each audience member gave.

I would then bring someone onstage and ask them to put on one of the uniforms and embody the identity of what the uniform represented. Then I'd ask them how they felt, and how they might approach some of the challenges they're currently dealing with. People always responded with something positive, and they felt they could deal with their sales calls, negotiations, husbands, children, or whatever else was going on in their worlds with more confidence.

As a fun exercise, I'd get them to show me how they would walk, how they would hold their head, how they'd stand, the looks on their faces. Basically, how would they behave? The audience got a laugh out of it, but the point was to show people how quickly we morph from role to role in our lives. Some powerful shifts would happen onstage.

In one instance, a young girl who had been bullied for years walked up to a group of girls she imagined on the right side of the stage while wearing the Wonder Woman outfit and called them out.

She even said afterward, "If I went and did that at school, they'd probably hit me. But I wouldn't care, because Wonder Woman could handle it."

On another occasion, while talking to a group of sales professionals for a large insurance company, a man picked up an imaginary phone and ran through his an entire "call script" perfectly while wearing the army uniform. When we unpacked the experience, he said, "It was like I could suspend all my worries about rejection, because there's no damn way a Navy SEAL is going to care about it." He went on to tell us, "I haven't been able to get through that script, ever. I forget parts of it because I'm so emotional. Now I know what I'm capable of."

It's incredible how quickly we can change our concepts of what's possible when we adopt a new identity, just as you've already read with previous research, examples, and studies I've outlined throughout the book. And now, with a "symbol" like a Totem, it'll be much easier to slip into your Alter Ego.

THE FORMULA FOR A POWERFUL TOTEM

The Totem embodies your Alter Ego's Superpowers, its Origin Story, and its mission. When that Totem is activated, it calls forth your Alter Ego. Just like the white coat changed the students.

School was always a challenge for me growing up. Not because I didn't like it, but because reading didn't make sense. I didn't know why, and I sure as heck didn't want to let anyone know I was "too stupid" to read. It forced me to be creative when teachers handed out reading assignments during class. I'd do my best to make my way through the reading assignment, and before the time was up, I'd start asking some of my friends around me what they thought about the passage. It got me labeled a "class clown," "disturber," or "talker," but it was my way of preparing myself just in case I was asked questions by the teacher.

Back then when I looked around the classroom at my peers, the smartest kids in my grade wore glasses. Plus, the most intelligent kids in my younger sister's class also wore glasses. Me? I had perfect vision.

So, I developed this view of the world, that smart people had glasses. Is it *absolutely* true? Of course not. But that was my experience and the meaning I attached to it. I wonder what views of the world you developed at a young age that have possibly shaped your world.

The equation in my head was simple: Glasses + People = Smart.

I ultimately found out in my twenties after a car accident, when I went in for psychological testing, that I was dyslexic. But the belief about smart people wearing eyeglasses had become ingrained in me.

When I was trying to launch my first business, I just couldn't close the deals. I knew I had something important to offer people. But I had this massive insecurity about looking like I was twelve years old with my baby face and that people wouldn't respect or listen to me.

Finally, a thought popped into my head from my school days: "The people that get respected are the people others see as smart. And the smartest people I know have glasses." It was at that moment I found my Totem. If I wore glasses, went my thinking, then people would see me as smart, and they'd respect me. I also was a huge Superman fan, and Superman wore glasses as Clark Kent, so to me, this made glasses even more powerful.

As soon as I felt the wingtips of my glasses brush against my temples, I did my "Reverse Superman." Superman took off his glasses to become "normal"; I put on my glasses to get my "Superpowers." Just wearing that pair of glasses caused me to morph into the most confident, strong, intelligent version of myself, a version that I knew was respected.

Now, did my potential clients actually believe I was smart? Did they actually respect me more than they had before? I don't know. I don't care. It didn't matter. Whether anyone associated intelligence and respect with a pair of eyeglasses wasn't the point. I was the one creating and living in my world, and if I felt more intelligent, more respectable, and more decisive, that was the only thing that mattered. Because emotion drives performance. And it worked.

WHY YOU NEED A TOTEM

Most people show up on their Field of Play without much thought or awareness about who needs to be there to produce an outstanding result. I've said this before, but we're always moving from one Field of Play to another and from one role to another. Each role requires different traits to perform at our highest level. Since we're unaware we're shifting into and out of roles, we end up bringing the same characteristics to each field.

Selecting and activating the Totem sets the intention of the specific traits you want to call upon in a particular Moment of Impact. It's like you're setting an internal compass so that you align your emotions, thoughts, and behaviors. You're being very intentional in tapping into the Heroic Self you need when you need it.

Remember the colonel I met at Fort Bragg when I was there giving a speech? He was struggling with being the kind of father he wanted to be with his kids after coming home in his army uniform (remember the power of "enclothed cognition"). His personality didn't change, even after changing into a pair of jeans and a golf shirt. To finish the story, I talked to him more about whom he respected as a parent, the qualities and traits he really wanted. And what he thought would make that "Field of Play" extraordinary. He mentioned how much he loved the actor and television host Mike Rowe, a man known for being self-deprecating, approachable, funny, and into doing pretty much anything. After all, he hosts a show called *Dirty Jobs*, which takes him into the worlds of people doing some of the smelliest, hardest, and filthiest jobs on the planet.

I agreed. I love Mike Rowe's personality, too.

There's something else Mike is known for: wearing a baseball cap. After I explained to the colonel the power of symbols, enclothed cognition, and using a Totem to Activate his Alter Ego, his eyes lit up. "My 'Dad Self' is wearing a cap."

THE POWER OF A PILL

When I initially began working with clients and helping them create an Alter Ego, I would bring a box of Tic Tacs. I'd have the label already torn off, hand them the container, and say, "Before you go on the field, take one of these little pills and imagine it contains the Superpower characteristics you want to Activate. But don't just pop it in your mouth. I want you to pause for a moment and really be deliberate about who is going to show up on the field."

Fast-forward to over fifteen years later and I've given out over thirty thousand "Alter Ego X Pills" to help clients Activate their Heroic Self. The placebo effect of taking a pill, with no pharmaceutical qualities, has been one of the most effective Totems I've seen clients use. The most common response from people, and one someone recently shared, was "I feel like it works from the inside out. Almost like it triggers a hidden power."

Even though you may use something as simple as a piece of candy, don't overlook the power of using this Activator to trigger your Alter Ego. (If you'd like to learn more about this placebo effect and the Alter Ego X Pill used by the community, go to AlterEgoXPill.com.)

SHIFT TO YOUR PHYSICAL WORLD

The Alter Ego is designed to transform your performance. That includes everything from how you physically act and behave to your thoughts to your emotions, your beliefs to your values, your posture to the tone of your voice. And all the way through the "layers" of the Alter Ego Effect Model.

Right now, the Alter Ego that will bring forth all these Superpowers and tap into your Heroic Self is lying dormant and ready to be Activated—it's in the realm of your imagination on the mental and emotional planes.

You need something that will call it forth into the physical world and into physical form.

That's what the Totem does. It gives your Alter Ego a form and a shape. It's not just an idea floating in your head or an emotion you feel. It's not just some vivid daydream that you distract yourself with in a meeting. Your Alter Ego is real, and it needs to be grounded in a physical presence.

A Totem engages more of your senses. You can feel, smell, taste, touch, and see the object, which sparks a visceral feeling.

Try this: Imagine walking to the fridge. Open the door, pull out a lemon, and place it on a cutting board. Now pull out a knife and cut a wedge or slice. Bring the lemon slice to your nose. Take a big whiff; what does it smell like? Cut another slice from the lemon. How does the juice feel on your fingers? Now bring a slice to your mouth and take a big bite of it. Did your mouth water a little? Did you pucker your lips?

Now try this. If you have a lemon in the fridge, go and actually grab it, and do everything I just had you imagine. See, feel, taste, and smell it.

Do you see the difference? Your imagination is undoubtedly powerful, but nothing compares to being able to experience it in the physical world. Your Alter Ego's Totem or Artifact is the bridge from your imagination to the physical world. It's the anchor.

Having this Totem to anchor your Alter Ego, too, not only enables the transformation, but it also helps leverage one of the core foundations of habit change. Cary Grant, the famed actor, who was born Archie Leach, said, "I pretended to be somebody I wanted to be, and I finally became that person. Or he became me. Or we met at some point." This is what the Alter Ego is designed to help you reach, this place where your Heroic Self naturally comes forth without having to think about it when you need it.

Eventually that happened to me. At first I'd put the glasses on and call myself Richard, until at some point I didn't need the name or the glasses to feel smart or respected or confident. I just was. I just started showing up that way in all my potential client meetings. It became a habit. I didn't need to intentionally call forth my best traits, because my best attributes had become ingrained. I'd created my new identity on the Field of Play of business. (By no means did this make me perfect! There was and still is work to be done, but it got me past the initial resistance I was struggling with.)

My goal as a performance coach is to help people get to the place where they consistently perform at their highest level, wherever that may be for someone. To do that, performance has to become a habit. It has to happen just as naturally as you breathe.

In the 1970s, Noel Burch created what remains a simplified model to explain the four stages of learning a new skill. It's called the Four Stages of Learning Competency, and it starts with someone being "unconsciously unskilled"; then you move to "consciously unskilled"; next, you become "consciously skilled"; and, finally, you are "unconsciously skilled."

I like to explain it in a slightly different way that shows the four stages of change we all go through.

Stage 1: Ignorance: You "don't know what you don't know." This is what is referred to as "unconscious incompetence." This is the classic stage of lack of awareness.

Stage 2: Awareness: You begin to realize that you "know you don't know" certain things. This is what's known as "conscious incompetence." You're aware you don't know how to do something.

Stage 3: Change: This is when "you know that you don't know" and you make the conscious decision to change. This is what's referred to as "conscious competence." This is the hardest stage because it's when the hard work happens, when you start changing habits, attitudes shift, and when you start to create new thought patterns inside your mind. This is where you know what to do, and you're doing it, but it's an effort because it's not ingrained yet.

Stage 4: Mastery: This is when the transformation is complete. It's where things become automatic for you. There isn't as much conscious attention. It's what's known as "unconscious competence." You know how to do it, and you don't need to think about it. It's one and the same, and every time you step onto your Field of Play, every time you face a Moment of Impact, your Heroic Self comes forth without thought.

Using your Totem helps to train you to call forth that Heroic Self. Over time, you may not even need your Totem; the choice is yours. I still like to wear my glasses, because I enjoy wearing them but also as a reminder to you and others that this is a natural part of life and being human.

We all have triggers. When I hear the song "Born to Run" by Bruce Springsteen, I'm transported back to driving on the Trans-Canada Highway in Medicine Hat, Alberta, with my buddy Bill, going to a weekend softball tournament. It's as clichéd as you can possibly get, but I hear that tune and I immediately get transported to summer in "the Hat" with my best friend.

It's the same idea when you put on a ring, wipe your face with a towel, or put on a uniform. Every time you engage with your Totem or Artifact, you're psychologically calling forth everything your Alter Ego embodies, from the traits you've selected to the backstory you've created to the mission you're on.

THE THREE TYPES OF TOTEMS OR ARTIFACTS

A Totem is merely the thing you're using to represent or connect to your Alter Ego or Field of Play. A white lab coat, a uniform, a hat, a pair of glasses, the stage or field itself. It could literally be anything.

An Artifact is the same thing, except it has some sort of historical significance. If you're using a piece of jewelry that has been handed down for generations, that's an Artifact. It has extra juice in it because of the historical connection to your ancestors or your tribe, or your family adds an additional level of significance to you.

This isn't something to get caught up in like a spiderweb; you don't need to sit there wondering if you should get an Artifact or a Totem. Their purpose is still the same, to activate your Alter Ego and carry the meaning of what you're doing. (For more inspiration, examples, and ready-made totems, go to AlterEgoEffect.com/totem.)

A Totem or Artifact is something you strongly associate with your Alter Ego, like a stethoscope and a doctor, Thor and his hammer, Wonder Woman and her golden lasso. The Totem or Artifact you select will be the physical embodiment of all the dominant traits you chose earlier in the book.

There are three types of Totem or Artifacts.

1. Something you wear

    This is the most potent Totem you could choose. You can slip it on or off, which, as you'll learn later, is crucial if you start to slide out of acting like your Alter Ego. This category includes just about everything and anything you can think of. Here are just a few ideas for where you can draw inspiration for your Alter Ego's Totem or Artifact.

Uniform	Jacket
Costume	Socks
Helmet	T-shirt
Hat (any type)	Bandana
Eyeglasses	Watch
Jewelry (e.g., a ring, necklace, bracelet)	Sweatshirt
	Pants
Wristband or sweatband	Shoes (e.g., sneakers, heels,
Suit	slippers, sandals)

2. Something you carry with you

    Tony, a baseball player, grew up on a farm in Iowa. His family is significant to him. His Alter Ego is motivated to make his family proud and to bring honor to his family's name. He carries a small pebble from his farm in his pocket, and every time he needs just a bit more juice from his Alter Ego, he slips his hand into his pocket and rolls the pebble around his fingertips.

    John is another example. He has a souped-up Artifact. His Alter Ego is his grandfather, and the Artifact is his grandfather's pocket watch. Some people will hold or carry a specific item, like a pen, when they're making sales calls or in an important meeting.

Here are other ideas for inspiration:

Cup (e.g., a coffee, tea, or travel mug)
Notebook
Baseball
Rock or pebble
Feather
Picture (e.g., of your Alter Ego or something that represents the traits of your Alter Ego)
Trading cards (like the ones I stuffed into my football uniform)
Special coin
Pen
Towel

When I was a teenager, I was a nationally ranked badminton player. I had this routine before every match of taking a white towel into the change room and placing it under the water faucet to make it wet. I'd wring it out so it wasn't dripping, fold it into a square about two feet each side, then place it on the side of the court.

The purpose to everyone else was to go over and place my court shoes on it, to get them wet and make them more sticky. But for me it was my "charging station." It's where I could "power up" my Alter Ego and return to the court with more energy.

As I've said, there are no rules to this. You can always add more dimensions to your Alter Ego's world, and using an additional Totem gave my Alter Ego more power.

Many clients have taken this exact method and used it, as well.

Remember Mitch? The finance guy taking on a new role? His Alter Ego was his inspirational grandmother that survived the Holocaust, immigrated to America, and raised four successful children. The Artifact he used was an old photo of his grandmother "from the homeland." He has it sitting on his desk, and whenever he feels like he's lacking confidence or is challenged by a situation, he turns the frame just slightly more toward him to "switch on" his grandmother's strength.

3. Something connected to the Field of Play

As soon as Bo Jackson stepped onto the football field, he transformed into Jason. The field was his Totem. For some of my Broadway clients, it's the stage. For one of my writing clients, it's every time he sits down in his writing chair. For a lot of my business clients, it's as soon as they step into the boardroom.

Your Totem doesn't have to be something that's on you, but it could be on the Field of Play or the Field of Play itself.

HOW TO CHOOSE YOUR TOTEM OR ARTIFACT

Above all, don't make this into a Halloween costume. Don't pick eight things and call them all your Totems. Pick one. Be selective. There are a few principles I'd go so far as to say are mandatory.

1. It must symbolize something to you.

Whatever you choose will be used to call forth your Alter Ego and all the Superpowers and Origin Story you've created. It's everything. It's the symbol of your Alter Ego, so make sure the two connect.

What you select may have an indirect connection to your Alter Ego, like my client who works on Wall Street whose Alter Ego is Batman. Now, there's no way he can show up dressed in a Batman suit and still keep his job. But he can get creative.

Batman dresses in black, so my client chose a black tie or a black suit as his Totem. He'd wear the tie or suit on days when he had to take an important meeting and knew he would need his Alter Ego.

Your Totem or Artifact may have a direct connection to your Alter Ego. I know one person who uses a pair of Superman cuff links. There's a collegiate golfer whose Alter Ego is Tiger Woods. He has golf-head covers striped like a tiger, and he wears a pair of socks with a tiger crest stitched onto them. One of my equestrian clients wears a custom-made bracelet, just like the one Wonder Woman wears.

Clients that choose animals or inanimate objects will often select a ring, pendant, earrings, or pretty much anything to invoke their "spirit animal." A client who plays professional soccer has an Alter Ego, "the Stealth Bomber." Why? Because "I'm hard to find, I'm fast, and by the time you know I'm there I've blasted a ball into the back of the net." He has special insoles in his shoes with a sticker of a real stealth bomber.

Your Totem may have no connection to your Alter Ego either. It could be a universal symbol, or it could hold meaning just for you. A pair of glasses was my Totem, but not everyone would associate respect and intelligence with a pair of frames like me.

Whatever you choose, be it directly connected to your Alter Ego or not, just make sure the emotional resonance and meaning are there for you.

2. Whatever you choose must be something you can always use on your Field of Play. No sometimes things!

One of my clients chose his physical environment for his Totem. He was a hockey player, and as we stepped on the ice he imagined his Alter Ego living inside a specific board on his hometown rink. Cool idea, except that it only worked during home games. If you're going to choose something, especially if it's on the Field of Play like walking into the boardroom, make sure it's something you can always use.

We merely adjusted my client's Alter Ego to be living on the ice, like Bo Jackson's lived on the field. Instead of picking a specific boardroom, it could be the simple act of walking through the entryway of a boardroom. So the entryway becomes the Totem.

3. It should be something you can quickly take off and put on, or put into your pocket or take out, or step onto or off of.

I'm giving you a spoiler here, but there will be times when you slip out of your Alter Ego, especially when you first start using it. You'll slide back into the old traits and Trapped Self that used to show up. When this happens, you need a reset. When I wore my glasses, if I started to get pulled into the Ordinary World by any of the forces the Enemy uses, like insecurity, fear, or worrying what others thought of me (those were my big three), I would take the glasses off. Richard never had those thoughts, so the glasses needed to come off. Just that simple act would remind me of what I was there to do, what was essential, and that Richard was capable of slaying those dragons and getting back on the Field. Then I'd put them back on.

After a while, simply feeling the frames glide across my temples would infuse me with confidence and trigger my Alter Ego to return again.

That's the reset.

If your Totem is a field or a boardroom, it's hard to step on and off at any moment. I won't go so far as to say don't choose the Field of Play, but just be mindful. If you select something on your Field of Play as your Totem, then be creative with how you'll reset and call forth the Alter Ego when you start to slip.

You can even borrow the idea I shared earlier about my folded towel on the side of the court. There could be a specific action or place you go to in that environment to "reset" or "power up."

One client takes their wedding ring and taps the boardroom table to invoke their Alter Ego to return and send the insecure thoughts back into the ether.

DANGER! AVOID THESE MISTAKES

The Alter Ego is simple. It's hard to build this incorrectly, but you can get turned around at this stage. Here's what *not* to do.

1. Don't wear, carry, or use the Totem or Artifact all the time. Your Alter Ego is built for a specific Field of Play, or you use it for those challenging Moments of Impact. You want to be intentional, and if you're always using the same Alter Ego across all the Fields of Life, then you're missing the point. You play different roles in different areas of your life, and each one has certain qualities that will help you more than others.

2. Don't give your Totem or Artifact away. This is for you and your Alter Ego. Don't lend it to someone, and I'd suggest not telling others about it. Sarah and Brandon who are sitting next to you in a meeting don't need to hear the real story about your Superman cuff links. Keep the power and knowledge secret. I'm only openly talking about the Alter Egos I've used in the past so I can illustrate certain points. Whether you keep your Alter Ego private from the people around you is up to you. However, in the beginning I recommend you do that. When you know something others don't, it gives you confidence.

   Also, if you're in competitive environments like sports or

sales, your competitors may end up trying to use it against you and trash-talk you. Now, that may be either bad or good, depending on your world. I just like to recommend keeping it tucked away initially. Your little secret.

3. Choose something you'll enjoy wearing or carrying or using. It should be something you have a positive association with. If you don't, then you'll strip it of any power.

ALWAYS HONOR THY ALTER EGO

When I was in high school, I would bring all the influences of my Alter Ego into a locker room I constructed in my mind. Walter Payton, Ronnie Lott, and Native American leaders. I would imagine having a conversation with them. One by one, each of them would hand me something. If you recall, I used to put the trading cards of Walter and Ronnie into my uniform. I imagined them handing me their cards, and Walter saying to me, "Todd, here is my card. Here's a bit of me that you get to put into your helmet, but don't you dare go out there and dishonor me by not giving it your absolute best. Attack every single player, no matter their size, and just know I'll be there with you to run right over them. And if you're not willing to do that, take that card outta there and give it back. Don't dishonor any of us by not honoring how we played and who we are."

Now, for some that may sound tough, but I was also creating an intense level of conviction and a space of honor. I was connecting deeply to my Alter Ego. That little conversation infused my Alter Ego with meaning. If I was going to embody these great football players and Native Americans, I'd better pay them the respect they deserve. I'd better honor their meaning.

Give your Alter Ego the honor and integrity it deserves. If your Alter Ego is your grandfather, a superhero, someone you admire, or an animal that you revere, are you really going to dishonor its name, its story, its legacy? I certainly hope not. That honor, that legacy, that respect and meaning are embodied in the Totem or Artifact.

Ziva David is a fictional character from the CBS show *NCIS*. She's a lethal Mossad agent, a former Israeli military operative, and she carries herself with a ton of confidence and always feels like she's on equal footing with men. Well, it turns out a few of my clients really resonate with her and have used her as their Alter Egos.

One from a top financial firm explained to me, "There wasn't a chance in hell I wasn't going to show up and be pushed around by any men. Ziva would kick my ass if I did."

Bottom line: commit.

THE ACTIVATION EVENT

This final part of the process is when you unite the Alter Ego, the Totem, and your Field of Play or Moment of Impact. Superman steps into the phone booth or tears open his shirt. Wonder Woman spins to transform into Wonder Woman. Spider-Man pulls on his mask. There's a moment when you deliberately step into this other form, your Alter Ego. The Activation Event is when you use the Totem or Artifact as a switch, signaling to your mind it's time for your Alter Ego to take over.

The easiest way to make this happen is to believe your Alter Ego lives inside the Totem or Artifact. The moment you swallow the Alter Ego X Pill, it's Activated. The moment you slip on the ring, it's Activated. The moment you slide the pebble or pocket watch in your pocket, it's Activated. The moment the arms of the glasses slip past your temples, it's like they're flicking a switch as they go by to Activate your Secret Identity.

In chapter 1 I introduced you to Anthony, the young athlete who took an early train to New York City and tracked me down for help.

Anthony was a rising star in Maryland high school basketball. He was always one of the best players on the court, until another player transferred to his school for senior year. The new guy was an all-star, and it didn't take long before Anthony started to second-guess himself and overthink his moves on the court. He began to worry that everyone in the stands was comparing him to the new kid and thinking he was just average now. Just as the young baseball player lost his ability to play the game, Anthony lost his edge and began to make mistakes. He desperately wanted to get his game back.

In the end, he chose a panther as his Alter Ego for its power, agility, and stamina. His Totem was a towel, and he Activated the panther just before the game started. Right after warm-ups were over, he went to the sidelines, reached in his bag, grabbed the towel, and deliberately wiped his face, as if he were pulling on a panther mask like Spider-Man. He imagined the mask acting like an exoskeleton. He didn't feel he was on display. He didn't worry about what people were thinking or saying. He was hidden. (To see an example of how to do this, go to AlterEgoEffect.com/towel to watch me demonstrate it.)

After he wiped his face, he would spring from the chair like a panther making a move on its prey.

It was time for his Alter Ego.

Wiping his face and springing from the chair was the trigger that Activated his Alter Ego and all his Superpowers.

When I put my glasses on, the moment I felt the wings slip across my temples and behind my ears was the moment I knew it was time to bring my Alter Ego out. For Alicia, a writer, she would sit on her writing chair and pull on her old college hoodie. For Lisa, the equestrian rider, she pulls on her custom-made Wonder Woman bracelet before climbing into the stirrups and swinging her leg over the saddle. For Tony, the baseball player from Iowa, he would reach into his pocket and pinch the pebble from his family's farm with his thumb and middle finger.

For my golf player, he pulled on his socks halfway up his calf, finished tying his golf shoes, then grabbed his socks and yanked them up to full length to "Activate Tiger." For another business client, his Totem and Activation Event happen when he puts on his Bruno Magli shoes. He starts with his right foot and ties the laces. Then he slides his left foot into his shoe, but before he plants the heel onto the insole, he pauses. He activates his Alter Ego with a slight stomp. If he ever feels like he's slipping back into old habits or losing the power of his Secret Identity, he taps his heels together "to wake up the beast inside."

By the way, the reason he uses his left foot to activate is that he used to be a great soccer player, and he was "deadly with the left foot."

Now, all of this could sound like children's games to some. "Stomping a foot," "yanking up socks," "playing with a pebble"—"That stuff's for kids, and I'm a grown adult!" And you're right. If that's your attitude, then go with it. It's just that you're denying science, you are denying the way your mind already works, and you're denying the way elite people live and perform. If you'd like to find a book on what average people do, there are hundreds of those already on the bookshelf.

I didn't invent the human imagination and the natural way we've magnified certain parts of our personalities in the past or played with characters in the past. A love of myths and archetypes is baked into us.

YOUR TURN

Remember, our Alter Ego isn't on 24/7 duty. The Activation Event could be the entire time you're on your Field of Play, or possibly just in specific Moments of Impact, where you stumble and don't show up as you want.

If you're a sales pro, maybe you want to use your Alter Ego throughout your entire day. Or perhaps you just want to use it when you need to "close the sale." If you're an athlete it could be the whole time you're competing on the field, or maybe in the final moments of a game or against a specific opponent or in a particular situation. If you're a business owner and marketing is your big challenge right now, maybe you only leverage the power of your Alter Ego during networking events, interacting on social media, or writing marketing materials.

In any of those cases, grab your Totem, know your Alter Ego is waiting for you, and Activate it. What you're looking for is a natural trigger you can pair with your Totem or Artifact. Every time I come home from my office, and before I step into our home, I pause, grab a bracelet my daughter made for me, and slide it on. Now it's time for the fun dad to show up, not the coach, businessman, or investor.

Keep the event simple and easy to perform and remember: just make sure the trigger you select is something you can always do.

If your Totem is a ball cap, the Activation Event would happen when you slide it on your head. It could be slipping on the piece of jewelry you chose, like a ring or a necklace. It could be the act of putting on a specific shirt or tie before a meeting. It could be picking up a special pen and clutching it in your hand. Another client wears a locket with a picture of her mother, and before a networking event, she'll open the locket, close it, and walk in. (For video examples, go to AlterEgoEffect.com/totem.)

Your Activation Event can be anything that feels natural and comfortable, but it has to be a physical action.

I've taught this process thousands of times to individuals and groups, and here's what I know. After seeing the whole picture and seeing how everything fits together in this final phase, things click. If that's you, then returning to some of the earlier chapters might help you deepen your connection to your Alter Ego and its purpose. Like I said before, each one of these components is like a doorway leading into the incredible world of using Alter Egos to achieve big or small goals, to have more fun, and to take more of the internal struggle out of life. So if seeing how a Totem or Artifact activates your Alter Ego made things click, work backward through the book or dive into other chapters to leverage its full power.

I've had clients say to me, "This is great, but what happens when I'm really doubting myself?" Or, "What do I do when I really start feeling the fear of moving forward?" Or, "I'm superintimidated by someone, and I can't get my Alter Ego to work, and I feel myself retreating back into the Trapped World you talk about."

Just like the Hulk, Wonder Woman, or Thor, you need a Ground Punch.

So let's get one . . .

CHAPTER 15

TESTS, TRIALS, AND DELIVERING THE GROUND PUNCH

There are moments in every superhero movie when the momentum swings, the Enemy is winning the day, and the Hero is close to defeat. However, from a place deep inside, the hero gathers their strength, harnesses another energy source, or finds a way to overcome the onslaught with a steely-eyed glare and a "This ends now!" rallying cry.

The crowd jumps to their feet, fists in the air and roaring with jubilation. Like in *Rocky III*, when Rocky is fighting the vicious James "Clubber" Lang, played by Mr. T. Rocky is taking a beating from the bigger fighter. It's looking like there's no way Rocky could win, when he suddenly roars back, nailing Clubber with a series of shots until finally finishing him with a stunning knockout blow. I was six years old sitting in the back row of the theater with my brothers Ross and Ryan, and I leaped out of my chair screaming when it all happened.

It's cliché. But clichés are clichés for a reason. They're true.

Everybody needs to know how to pull out of a spiral and come back to win.

You know how the Incredible Hulk smashes his fists into the ground, creating a seismic shock wave that knocks out the Enemy? And you ask yourself: Why did he wait so long to do it? That's what you need: a Ground Punch.

In the 2017 *Wonder Woman* movie, the final fight scene involves the villainous god Ares, revealing his plans to destroy humanity and urging Wonder Woman to join him. During the battle, her friend and ally, Steve, sacrifices himself to save everyone from a lethal bomb. The mighty Ares tries to convince her again that humanity needs to be destroyed. However, Diana sees her friend's sacrifice as an example of the best that humankind possesses. She refuses to join Ares and finds the strength inside herself to redirect Ares's lethal lightning bolt attack back at him, destroying him once and for all.

You can find these moments in almost every movie, and I'll bet there are moments in your own life when you "dug deep," "found another gear," or "refused to give up."

So let's make sure you can always find that extra gear when you need to.

A TENNIS PLAYER'S BATTLE

Weekends are hectic when you're working with athletes. On this particular Saturday, it was no different. I rolled over and picked up my phone off my side table to see if anything had come through from some clients I had competing on the other side of the globe. I saw three notifications from Rachel.

Rachel was one of the tennis players I mentioned earlier in the book, who struggled with sabotaging her dominance on the court. Fairness was one of her core values, but on the court it would cause her to feel bad for opponents she was beating badly. That meant she'd "let up" and allow them to get back into the game—not the best strategy in sports.

Rachel was over in Asia playing in a tennis tournament, so I unlocked my phone to see what was going on. Judging by her messages, it looked like her Alter Ego was failing her.

I snuck out of bed, trying to leave the pile of little kids that had made their way into our room in the middle of the night undisturbed, and crept out into the living room. I tapped her name on my phone and gave her a call.

"Hello."

"Hey, Rachel, what's up?" I asked.

"Well, like I said in my messages, I was in the middle of my match yesterday, playing great. Totally committed to the process and competing hard on every shot. When I felt like I was starting to lose my edge, I tried to power through it with my Alter Ego, but it just wasn't working."

"What happened with the match?" I asked.

"I was ahead by a lot, so I pulled it out in the end, but it took forty minutes longer than it should have. Plus, she wasn't very good."

"Okay, this is something we can fix. So don't get stressed out over it."

I went on to ask her if she was getting trapped in the old habits of getting on the "merry-go-round" of negative self-talk. Rachel thought about it for a moment, then said, "No, I think I just got caught up in the old pattern."

"Great," I said. "Let me show you how to use a Ground Punch, to knock any doubt, negativity, fear, or worry flat on its ass."

"A *Ground Punch*?" she asked.

I shared with Rachel how to use a Ground Punch to keep her confidently moving forward with a deep conviction to achieving her mission. I want to show you two different methods you can keep tucked into your Alter Ego's armory, ready to use when the Enemy approaches and tries to pull you off course.

I had you make a note of how your Alter Ego moves, how it speaks, how it feels, how it thinks, and its mannerisms. You created its Origin Story and chose a Totem or Artifact. This wasn't just a mental or emotional exercise. You also thought about the behavioral changes and physical actions your Alter Ego will adopt.

Once the Activation Event happens, then your Alter Ego is called forth, and the physical, mental, and emotional transformation should be complete, right? Yes. But that doesn't mean it's all sunshine and rainbows.

Let's go back to Rachel. We worked through this entire process together to find, develop, and activate her Alter Ego. She began using it, having fun with it, and getting results. But just like any Hero, things don't always go your way; unexpected situations arise, or that dreaded Enemy shows up to pull you away from your mission.

Wonder Woman can have all the speed, skill, and power in the world, but even she gets challenged by outside forces and internal forces. Enemies show up to stop her, the game she thought she was playing changes suddenly because a villain throws a wrinkle into her plans, or old thoughts from her past creep in to cast doubt on what she could or should achieve.

What does she do?

She delivers a devastating Ground Punch!

It's that "Not here, not now!" moment. Or the steely glare that wards off an enemy's advance. It's your deep inner commitment to being the Heroic Self.

PUTTING THE ENEMY IN ITS PLACE

We're continually having conversations in our heads. The conversation can switch to becoming unsupportive and unhelpful when you're trying to undertake a challenge. Right now, maybe there are elements of your identity that aren't set up to help you win on the Field of Play. There's a part of your world that we've named your Enemy, and it shows up and causes you to stumble. It causes you to hesitate, over-think, or doubt yourself.

Creating the Alter Ego initiates a healthy conversation in your head. Before creating the Alter Ego, maybe the only voice you heard on this particular Field of Play was critical, judgmental, and aimed at convincing you to play it safe. Because you've gone through the process of giving the Enemy a name, like Valeria did when she named the Enemy Igor, and you've created this Alter Ego and given it a name, you've created a clear duality. You're no longer living in a world where the conversation in your head is with "yourself" and getting caught in a "merry-go-round" conversation that doesn't lead anywhere.

The Alter Ego and the Field of Play it's operating on create a divid-ing line with the Enemy. And now you can talk to the Enemy when it shows up to pull you into the sidelines of life, where you become a spectator. Make no mistake, the Enemy is a part of us, and it's never going to vanish from existence. However, now you have this potent force to combat it, the Alter Ego.

So how do you deliver your "Ground Punch"? How do you put the Enemy in its place? You use one of these two methods proven to be effective over an extended period.

GROUND PUNCH 1: THE CURB KICK

The Curb Kick is the equivalent of kicking the Enemy to the curb or sidelines. It's precisely what I used with Rachel, the tennis player. Her Enemy's name was Suzie. That was the name of a character from a book she read once and whom she disliked.

During our call I told her that every time she caught herself slipping into old behaviors and feeling like she was about to let an opponent come from behind, her Alter Ego would have a quick conversation with Suzie, saying:

"Hey, Suzie, this is my fucking court. Get the hell to the sidelines.

That's where you live. This right here? This court. This is my home. I fucking live here. Now get outta here!"

Yes, it's intense. But it was incredibly useful, not only for Rachel but for the hundreds of other people who have used it. One comment from a friend of mine I shared this with: "I finally feel like I own the space between my ears." Rachel sent a strong message about who was supposed to be showing up at that moment and what she's there to do.

Another client of mine had a different approach; he imagined his Enemy as being a hyper puppy always wanting to distract him and procrastinate by doing fun things and avoiding doing the hard stuff. He named his Enemy Beagle. Anytime he had this pull to avoid the work he felt called to do, he would say:

"Beagle, I see what you're doing. This isn't play time. Find someone else to bother. I'm doing vital work right now, which is building a future I'm excited about. Beat it."

When we put names or attach personas to the conversations we're having in our heads, we create constructive conversations, like what Rachel was doing. It prevents our minds from getting entangled in our thoughts and instead gives us perspective and a path forward.

It's almost like a bright EXIT sign appears in our minds, giving us the chance to get back to what we want.

GROUND PUNCH 2: YOUR RESPONSE PROCLAMATION

Over the years that I've been teaching the Alter Ego Effect, I've never had one elite athlete or leader object to the idea. I've never had anyone tell me they feel like they're being fake or even childish. Most of them felt it to be one of the most natural things they could do or had already been doing. Now, they can battle with thoughts that don't serve them, just like you. No human is immune to the Enemy.

If you hear a little voice telling you, "You're being fake," or "This is silly," or "There's no use, you can't change," or "Who do you think you are? You don't have any talent or skill, and you're not going to make it," understand this: that's the Enemy trying to pull you back into the shadows where mediocrity lives.

It doesn't matter how many wins you tuck under your belt; your Enemy is always going to try to stop your Heroic Self from coming forward. Whether I'm talking on the phone to an alpine skier while they're lying in their tiny dorm room in the Olympic village the night before their event, or speaking with an MLB baseball pitcher twenty-nine minutes before he heads onto the mound in front of forty-eight thousand fans for a key playoff game, high-performing, successful, talented people still get tripped up by their Enemy asking them, "Who do you think you are?"

There will still be times while you're on your Field of Play that the Enemy will get the upper hand. This is when we lay down an earth-shattering Ground Punch to the internal question, "Who do you think you are?"

I call it a "Response Proclamation." And it's our way of finding that second gear, by having a well-prepared response to the question, "Who do you think you are?" or any question in similar form to cause you to doubt yourself. This not only prevents you from getting on the "merry-go-round" of negative self-talk; it also causes you to stay rooted in your Moment of Impact as your Heroic Self or your Alter Ego.

A Response Proclamation is the weapon your Alter Ego needs. Here's what a Response Proclamation sounds like for my Olympic alpine skier.

"Who am I? Who am I, you ask?

"I'm the one that's woken up at 4:18 a.m. every day for 1,123 straight days to be the first one on the ski hill to get my reps in for this moment.

"Who am I?

"I'm the one who spends forty-five minutes every day, lying on my back relaxed and confidently seeing and experiencing myself race down this hill and execute the tight turns with strong legs and great form so I give myself the best chance to put up a time that may just win me a medal.

"Who am I?

"I'm the one that some little kid, sitting at home, cross-legged, mesmerized and staring at his TV set, is going to point at and look over his shoulder to Mom and say, 'I'm gonna be like them someday, Mom.'

"I'm the one powered by a force far greater than anything you can throw my way. So, excuse me if I don't have time for your bullshit question because this life I've got is bigger than some question based in fear.

"So why don't you get your ass to the sidelines where you belong!"

It shines a light on the Enemy, sending it slinking off into the corner, curling up into a ball, sucking its thumb and crying for mommy, just like most bullies do.

This Ground Punch is there to knock the Enemy on its ass.

CRAFTING YOUR RESPONSE PROCLAMATION

A few years ago I shared a video of the Response Proclamation on Facebook, and shortly after, a client of mine named Mark reached out to schedule a call. He wanted help creating his.

An excellent Response Proclamation spotlights your grit, your hustle, and your achievements. I'm going to walk you through what I did with Mark, and as you read it, imagine you were Mark, and we were having this conversation.

Go back in time to the beginning of your career. Tell me the story of your life, told through the lens of your wins and accomplishments. I know you have them. You wouldn't be reading this book if you hadn't already tasted success—you want to taste more of it, and with more consistency.

Mark runs a successful e-commerce business that hit a rough patch. A good portion of his business goes through Amazon, and recent changes the company had made had caused Mark to worry that he couldn't pivot fast enough to adjust. He also launched a new service where he taught other entrepreneurs how to build successful e-commerce businesses. Mark would host live events to share the ins and outs of what worked for him. He had developed massive insecurity that he was an imposter. He questioned whether he had anything of value to share with other entrepreneurs, especially when he wasn't sure if his business could survive Amazon's changes.

"When you look at your career . . ." I began. I needed to take Mark out of his Ordinary World, where his Enemy was tugging on the thread of imposter syndrome, so we took a more holistic look at his career. I'd ask him a question, and he'd slowly tell me stories of his past, almost like an autobiography. Then I would repeat back to him what I'd hear.

"So, let me get this straight," I told him. "You started your professional career as a police officer in Miami. What was your next move?"

"I sold photocopiers."

"Interesting, so you became pretty good at that, huh? It must have taken you a long time to become successful since you started your career as a cop and not a salesman."

"Well, no, it took me eight months before I became the top photocopier salesperson in Florida."

"Wow, that's no time at all! What did you do after selling photocopiers?"

"Well, one of my clients was ordering a ton of stuff from my company, more than just photocopiers. I wanted to know what they were doing, so when I showed up at his office, it was filled with a bunch of twenty-six-year-olds with Lamborghinis in the parking lot. They were selling prepaid cards door-to-door to grocery and convenience stores. I took one look at them and thought, If these kids can do it, so can I."

"So, were you good at that, too?" I asked.

He chuckled. "Yeah, I guess so. I was doing a million dollars a month in that business until the technology sector broke through and made calling cards obsolete."

"Okay, so what did you do next?" I was trying to get him to see all the wins he had under his belt.

"I saw this ad on how to build e-commerce businesses for Amazon. I watched the video and thought, I can do this, and within six months, I was doing a million-plus a year."

"Okay, so let me get this straight. You're telling me, right now, you feel insecure because Amazon is constantly evolving and changing and you don't know if you can evolve or change with it?"

"Yeah."

"But the only thing I heard from your story is that you're great at evolving and changing."

He laughed and said, "Yeah, I guess you're right. Maybe I don't need a Ground Punch."

"No, you can still use the Ground Punch and Response Proclamation. The next time you hear that little voice inside your head, asking "Who am I to do X?" or saying "You can't do this" or "This isn't going to work out," you need to respond with:

"Who am I? Who am I, you ask?

"I'm the guy who left a job as a cop with no business experience, no sales experience and rose to be the number one salesperson in the entire state of Florida selling photocopiers door-to-door.

"Can't do this? I'm the guy who recognized an opportunity when I saw some freaking wet-behind-the-ear kids driving Lamborghinis, selling calling cards door-to-door, and went out and launched that business and made it a multimillion-dollar enterprise.

"It's not going to work out? I'm the guy who, when that rug got pulled out from underneath him, went and started another business in e-commerce. Oh, and by the way, I took that across the seven-figure threshold, too.

"If you think you're talking to a guy who can't reinvent himself, go knock on another door, because that ain't me."

I get chills every time I work on someone's Response Proclamation.

Now, that's one way to craft a Response Proclamation and lay down a Ground Punch to send a seismic shock wave through your nervous system and wake you up. Or you can craft your response from the perspective of the Alter Ego you've just worked hard to create.

So if you chose a character from movies, television, or literature, your response would be from that persona. If you chose an animal, your response would be influenced by the attributes of that animal. If it was a machine . . . you get the idea.

Imagine completely embodying the history and traits of Muhammad Ali or Oprah or Churchill or Nikola Tesla or any of the millions of possible permutations you could be influenced by.

When things became challenging, that Alter Ego responded in their voice, bringing you back onto the Field of Play.

So, how could you respond with a Ground Punch, sending a message that you won't pull away from your mission? That you won't hide and you're here to stay?

Write out a Response Proclamation in response to the question, "Who do you think you are?" Or, "This isn't going to work for you . . ." Or, "You can't do this . . ."

Remember, it can be from your history or your Alter Ego's history. Have fun with it and don't be afraid to be lethal with your response.

After you've created yours, I want to read it. Post it online and tag me. Or go to the AlterEgoEffect.com and follow the link to our community. There's nothing like being inspired by people who are out there, chasing their dreams, battling the Hidden Forces, and succeeding.

We're coming to the end of the journey of creating an Alter Ego you can use on any Field of Play in life. However, before we end this process, I have a few final tips to help you get the most out of this.

CHAPTER 16

MINDSETS, MISSIONS, QUESTS, AND ADVENTURES

"Do you want to see her?" This was the question Marilyn Monroe teasingly asked the photographer following her on the streets of New York.

Robert Stein recounted the story after spending a day with Marilyn Monroe in 1955 when their publication wanted to capture the non-Hollywood version of Marilyn.[1] She wrapped herself in a camel's hair coat, subdued her famous bouncy curls, and they walked her through Grand Central Terminal and down to the subway. Nobody paid any attention to her. Even while the photographer snapped photos of her hanging on to the strap dangling from the subway car, she went unnoticed. She was just Norma Jean, another passenger on the subway.

When they left the subway and came back up onto the street, Robert recounted, she turned to them and said, "Do you want to see her?" She proceeded to "take off her coat, fluff up her hair, arch her back and strike a pose."

Throngs of people swarmed her immediately.

This is the magic of the Alter Ego. You create your world. You decide who shows up on your Field of Play. And you decide what Superpowers and characteristics you'll bring into your world, to get the results you want.

Throughout this book you've read about people from the worlds of sports, business, and regular life who used Alter Egos to change their lives, overcome challenges, and chase down goals with more freedom. You've read about the multiple studies and mounting research that shows this approach not only helps you perform better, and helps you cope with life's natural challenges, but also taps into how we are all naturally wired to function.

You've learned that the Alter Ego Effect helps you tap into motivation and mindset behind why you're doing an activity, which draws you into an Extraordinary World.[2]

You've learned that by just wearing a white lab coat or choosing a Totem or Artifact to represent your Alter Ego, you immediately change your performance capabilities through the phenomenon of "enclothed cognition."[3]

You've learned that by identifying your deeper character traits and values to create your Superpowers, you act with more purpose and conviction.[4]

Now it's time to get you onto the Field of Play and have you experience the Extraordinary World more often.

The following is a series of quests or challenges to get you started and help you step into your Alter Ego and test its strength. They're designed to be simple and easy to execute. Plus, they're a fun way to experiment with your newly created Superpowers.

QUEST 1: THE COFFEE SHOP

Your first quest will be to go to a local coffee shop as your Alter Ego, order a favorite drink, and drink it as your Alter Ego.

For some people, as soon as they call forth their Alter Ego, it's like putting on their favorite pair of jeans. For others, their Alter Ego needs more breaking in. Some people need to practice what it feels like becoming their Alter Ego even before they step onto their Field of Play.

If that's you, then I encourage you to start practicing right now. The more you embody your Alter Ego, the Superpowers, the Origin Story, the easier it will be for you to bring this Heroic Self to your Moment of Impact.

HOW TO DO IT

Drive or walk to a local coffee shop and before you walk through the door, Activate your Alter Ego with your Totem or Artifact. Feel the change happen and walk through the door. Walk to the counter, order your drink, and sit down at a nearby table or walk back outside and drink your beverage of choice.

As you do this, be mindful of how you'd consume the drink as your Alter Ego; how would you hold it, sip it, stand, sit? Would you enjoy it differently? What will your Alter Ego be noticing about the surroundings, the people, and the environment? Will you be interacting with people differently? And how will the Alter Ego be feeling?

WHY THIS WORKS

It's a meaningless situation with no threat to your world. I'm not asking you to go and close the biggest deal of your life or do something terrifying or dangerous. You're just ordering a drink. The less stress around the activity or the more familiarity you have of the simple routine, the easier it will be for you to step into the playful side of the Alter Ego, without worrying about performing a difficult task.

A SIMPLE VARIATION

Go for a walk as your Alter Ego. Employ the same strategies as the "Coffee Shop Quest," and practice fully embodying your Alter Ego.

How would you feel about the world around you as your Alter Ego? Use the same questions I outlined in the coffee shop example to prompt you to activate your Alter Ego.

QUEST 2: THE NUMBER FOCUS GAME

This quest is designed to test your ability to focus and immediately test the powers of your Alter Ego. For twenty years, I've been teaching athletes the power of meditation and helping them develop stronger focus and concentration skills. It's hard to argue with the mountains of research on the benefits of meditation, but for some, they still didn't know if it was helping, so I developed a simple technique to close the feedback loop more quickly.

HERE'S HOW IT WORKS

Sit in a comfortable position. It could be in a chair or on the floor. Place an object like a ball or a blank piece of paper two feet in front of you. Set a timer for three minutes. During the three minutes, you'll start by visualizing the number 1, on the object. The moment you notice your mind has drifted off of the number 1, visualize the number 2 on the object. Once again, when you've noticed your mind has drifted, visualize the number 3. Continue this pattern until the timer goes off. Whatever number you're left with when the timer goes off is the number you'll want to record somewhere, like a notepad or in a note on your phone. If you ended with the number 34, then that's your score for this round. You want a lower number next round.

Now do the exercise again, except this time activate your Alter Ego with your Totem and go through the same process as your Alter Ego. If it's Einstein, be Einstein. If it's an elephant, be an elephant. If it's your strong and resilient grandmother, be her. Then record the number you're left with at the end.

How did it go? Were you better? Was it harder?

The two most common experiences of people trying this for the first time are: 1) they were able to beat their previous score by a fair margin; 2) they found themselves looping back and forth between remembering to be their Alter Ego and focusing on the number.

Either one is a great outcome because, with even more practice, things improve.

WHY THIS WORKS

Practicing becoming your Alter Ego and giving it a task to perform under slight competition is no different than athletes practicing and refining their skills, building endurance, strength, stamina, agility, and flexibility long before game day. Take a page from their books. If your Alter Ego's posture changes, practice it. Practice sitting straight in a chair instead of slouching. Practice a particular look in your eye, like a slight squint, because you're "dialed in" and focused.

There are no rules, except practice.

QUEST 3: PLAY A GAME

This quest is designed to have you experiment with your resiliency as your Alter Ego. Games and competitions are a great way to see someone's real personality. There's an old adage that an hour of play reveals more than a year of conversation. I agree. That is why this is a great test of the strength of your Alter Ego.

HOW TO DO IT

Choose a game to play with friends or family; play a video game on your favorite gaming device or put together a puzzle. By the way, nobody you're playing with needs to know about your secret identity.

Compete *as* your Alter Ego. The challenges, competition, or frustrations are a great way to flex your resilience muscle and truly get to know and embody your Alter Ego.

WHY THIS WORKS

A client of mine said, "I quickly realized how much more work I needed to do with my Alter Ego on getting past defeats. My personality has always been to take things way too personally when I'd lose. The first time I played a game as my Alter Ego, I let too much of my old self show up. It made me realize just how much I wanted to be my Alter Ego and rid myself of that negativity. And it worked. The more I became my Alter Ego, the less I ever cared about losing, which meant I started winning way more. It felt liberating."

Try this quest to test your resiliency and commitment. As you may recall from the chapter on the Enemy, it loves to use the forces of fear, judgment of others, and pride to pull you away from being your best. This will help you bubble it up to the surface, so you can slay those dragons before you'll need to defeat them in a Moment of Impact.

I mentioned it in the chapter on Totems and Artifacts, and it's worth repeating: when you slip, reset. This means taking off your glasses and putting them back on. Putting down your pen and picking it back up. It means removing the ring and placing it back on to switch back on. It means pulling the pebble out of your pocket and placing it back in again.

Tip: If you picked the Field of Play as a Totem, and you find yourself needing regular resets, consider changing to one that you can wear or carry with you.

The reset is a trigger for your mind, reminding you that there are specific Superpowers that you want and need to use in this precise moment. Being conscious and intentional is just another way to be your best coach out on the field.

FIND YOUR ALLIES

When you reflect on your life and any changes you've made, you probably felt uncertainty at first but then discovered a lot of the concerns were unnecessary. I agree with James A. Garfield: "I remember the old man who said he had a great many troubles in his life, but the worst of them never happened."

What I've experienced personally, and in the lives of countless men and women, is that allies are waiting to help you out. Despite what is played over and over again on loop in the media, the vast majority of people are kind, helpful, and generous—when given a chance. So find a tribe of allies to help you reach your mission, whatever it may be, and here are some places to start.

Allies that get you. Go to AlterEgoEffect.com and connect with a community of people already raising their hands and building Heroes and Heroines. There's tremendous power in finding other people who get the insider language we've used throughout the book. It's also easier for new friends to encourage each other and strategize change, because unlike some current friends or family, they aren't threatened by any of the changes being made. Sometimes your best allies will be new allies.

Allies you know. People in your existing world always have your back. Share with them what you're doing. Buy them the book or tell them about it and recruit them into the Extraordinary World. When people start to do things together for positive purposes, it creates something scientists call "upward spiral."[5] This upward spiral triggers a biological support structure that causes people to become closer, perform better, and be more likely to help each other out.

A corporate sales consultant shared this in an email to me a few years ago: "Bringing someone along in my 'secret world' has not only caused us to be great coaches for each other and accountability partners, but it's also been a lot more fun. We're beating our sales numbers every month, and any time one of us doesn't act like our Heroic Self, we call each other on it. It's turned work into a bit of a game."

Allies that mentor you. This has been one of the most significant strategies of my life. I've actively sought out mentors to learn from, apprentice with, and be pushed by since the beginning. Harvey Dorfman, one of the most respected mental game coaches on the planet, was one of my first great mentors. He was my Obi-Wan Kenobi. In fact, in Major League Baseball, he was known as the "Yoda of Baseball."

Now, you don't necessarily tell your mentor about your Alter Ego, but you can view them as that special wizard who shows up to help you realize your Extraordinary World. The great thing about this strategy is they can come in many forms. You can read their books or books about them and imagine them coaching you, talking you through a problem, or showing up when you could use some extra support. Or, they could be true mentorships, and you could meet with them regularly or semiregularly to get guidance and advice.

To this day I've had at least eleven true mentors I've met with on a consistent basis, and countless others who were "mentors from afar." They didn't know they were my mentor, but they took up residence in my mind and helped to guide me. Don't underestimate the power of a great mentor, because few things will impact you more.

By far and away, what holds a lot of people back is the fear of a new life in the Extraordinary. They think they'll leave behind the people they've spent their entire lives with. Joanne explains this best: "I grew up poor, and I vowed to myself to never be freaking poor. But, I felt like my family of origin, my parents and brothers, didn't understand. I was going after something different than everyone in my family. I wanted more for myself in ways they didn't.

"The moment I stepped out and used my Alter Ego to go after what I wanted, a new tribe showed up. It's amazing who you find when you start to go after big things!"

I love Joanne's raw honesty because it hits on what so many people fear: getting bounced from their tribes and failing to realize another one will show up.

What I've seen, personally in my life, and in the lives of countless men and women, is that when you leave one tribe, you find a new one. Or the new one finds you. Nature abhors vacuums. Empty a closet, and it'll fill back up again. Clean off a desk, and stuff will find its way back onto it. Dig a hole in the ground, and water or something else will find its way in. You may have to find your tribe. You may have to spend time in new places, join new groups, and make new friends, but I promise, you won't wander in the desert or jungle or Arctic tundra alone.

Calling forth your Alter Ego is a continuous process. Go, be playful, and collect the data. See what works and what doesn't for your Alter Ego. You may find you need a stronger Origin Story, or you need different Superpowers, or a different Totem or Artifact or a different Activation event. Maybe you need to craft a stronger Response Proclamation, or you need a better name.

Only you will know if something's not working. Merely find a balance between giving something a chance and then tweaking it for a more powerful result.

You can refine any part of the Alter Ego process, too. Maybe you realize you need another Superpower. Perhaps you realize you need a different Totem and Artifact. Don't be afraid to make changes if you need to.

SIX MINDSETS TO WIN

You've built an Alter Ego to carry you into your Extraordinary World. As you venture forth into the unknown, I have one final challenge. I challenge you to embrace these six principles. Think of them as reminders, as parting words, as inspiration, motivation, guidance, or advice. I have no idea what you'll find, but I know if you can allow these principles to guide you, then you'll see you can face any challenge.

1. Bring It On! (Embrace the Challenge)

   If there's something that separates pros from amateurs in any domain of life, it's the willingness to welcome obstacles and embrace challenges. Pros see them as a force that will make them stronger, sharpen their skills, and make them more valuable.

   Your Extraordinary World will challenge you, and if you face it with an openness and willingness to be challenged, then you'll find yourself developing more of the next Mindset . . .

2. I'm Ready for Anything! (Stay Flexible and Adaptable)

   When you have a willingness to be challenged, it opens up more of your mind so you can stay ready for anything. In sports, we call it active readiness. It keeps your mind open to creatively problem solve and helps you develop agility. It's also terribly intimidating to the Enemy. It's hard for any bully to deal with a foe standing in front of it who says, "I'm ready for anything you've got!" That's typically not a fight it wants.

3. I'm a Creative Force! (Embrace Your Imagination and Creativity)

   The more you embrace challenges, and stay flexible, the more you free up the mental space to be creative. You were born pretending and making believe and creating worlds in your head that don't exist in reality. Then you were told by the grown-ups to "stop doing that," "don't act that way," or to "grow up."

   But the "grown-ups" were wrong. Use your imagination; don't keep it hidden. It's a powerful tool that not only brings your Alter Ego to life, but unleashes its Superpowers, too.

4. I Love to Play! (Keep a Playful Attitude)

   Throughout the book, we talked about big, important things in our lives that matter to us—dreams and goals and pursuing worthy ideals. It's only natural that we take this stuff seriously. It's serious because the desire to achieve gnaws at us until we take action. But nobody says this can't also be fun.

We love games because they challenge and test us. Games bring out our playful sides (and our competitive sides, because let's face it, who doesn't like to win?). Games are fun, even when they challenge us.

We can be playful with the Alter Ego concept. The more playful you are, the better your results may be. Why? Because you'll be more likely to experiment, to take the Alter Ego you create into the field and see if it works. Then you'll tinker with it to make it even stronger, testing the results again, then tinkering some more, until you've found the best Alter Ego for you.

5. I Wonder What Will Happen?! (Appreciate Discovery and Curiosity)

What would happen if you approached your life like a mad scientist in a lab, willing to always test out new things to see if they'll work? What if every test in life was you answering the question, "I wonder . . . ?" What if you ended up finding out how truly capable you are with the help of your Alter Ego? You'll never know the answer unless you first answer the question, "I wonder . . . ?"

6. I Believe I Can Change! (Know You Can Reshape Your Mind)

Our personalities are malleable. We can reshape ourselves. We can change our beliefs and create new habits. We can change our identities. That's what the Alter Ego does for us. It helps us to tap into dormant capabilities and traits that we just haven't used, or haven't used in a setting that we want and need them in. If you've acted indecisively at work, you can learn to act decisively. If you've acted timidly during one-on-one meetings with prospective clients, you can learn to act assertively. If you've been awkward during networking events, you can learn to be poised.

Through her research, renowned psychologist Carol S. Dweck has found that success in any field—sports, business, the arts, in life—can be "dramatically influenced by how we think about our talents and abilities." She found two types of people in this world: those with a "fixed mindset," who didn't believe their abilities were capable of changing, and those with a "growth mindset," who believed their abilities could be developed. Guess which group found greater success? If you said the growth mindset crowd, you win.

Believing you can change how you show up on your Field of Play is crucial to successfully using the Alter Ego. You first have to think that change is possible. You have to believe that you can reshape those Moments of Impact and achieve an entirely new result.

CROSSING THE THRESHOLD

The famous professor, researcher, and mythologist Joseph Campbell popularized the concept of "the Hero's Journey." In his book *Hero with a Thousand Faces*, he explains:

"A hero ventures forth from the world of common day into a region of supernatural wonder: fabulous forces are there encountered, and a decisive victory is won: the hero comes back from this mysterious adventure with the power to bestow boons on his fellow man."[6]

George Lucas famously rewrote *Star Wars* after he discovered Campbell and his explanation of the Hero's Journey. He was even featured in the 1988 PBS documentary series *Power of Myth*, hosted by Bill Moyers. According to George Lucas, recorded in a later interview,[7] Campbell's teachings took an unusable five-hundred-page script and revealed in a simple model how the entire story needed to be laid out, because it followed a story arc repeated thousands of times throughout history's most celebrated stories, fables, and myths.

"It's possible that if I had not run across him, I would still be writing *Star Wars* today," Lucas said.[8]

There's a point in the Hero's Journey where the Hero has to "Cross the Threshold." It's the moment they leave their Ordinary World and set out on a new adventure. In *Star Wars*, it's when Luke Skywalker goes with Obi-Wan Kenobi to Mos Eisley and leaves his family farm. In *The Lord of the Rings*, it's when Frodo leaves the Shire and embarks on his quest to destroy the ring. In the 2017 *Wonder Woman*, it's when Diana leaves the hidden island of Themyscira to help save humanity.

In each case, there's an adventure, quest, or mission to be undertaken. Sometimes it's made by choice, and sometimes it's been chosen for them, whether by circumstance or a deep desire to fulfill some destiny.

Now, whether you picked up this book to

chase after a big goal like running a marathon,
navigate a significant change like starting a new career,
pursue a lifelong dream of writing a book,
make small changes like learning to cook,
embrace a new mindset like being confident when its time to
    close the sale, or
lead a life with more playful creativity,

the next step is to "cross the threshold" and begin.

At the end of your life, you won't remember the thoughts or intentions you had. You'll remember the actions you took. You'll judge yourself by how you showed up, by what you did, what you said, how you acted, and whether you performed the way you knew you could in any of the stages of life.

Just like any coach, when you hear the buzzer sound, I want you to look back and say, "I left nothing behind. I gave it my all. I did everything I wanted to do, and more important, I showed up as my Heroic Self with all my capabilities, skills, and intentions. And it toppled dominos, which changed my life in extraordinary, unpredictable ways. And because I did this, I lived a full life."

I know an Alter Ego can help make this happen.

I've waited fifteen years to write this book because I didn't want to write an anecdotal book of "Here's how I did it and you can, too" or "Here's a neat idea." I wanted to give you a template proven out by hundreds and thousands of clients, research, science, and history. There's comfort and confidence in knowing you're not only part of a tribe, but you're also just being human. Relish in the knowledge that your Alter Ego is helping to bring the very best version of yourself forward onto your Field of Play and into those Moments of Impact.

Use the Alter Ego to unlock that door to your Extraordinary World, to that part of you waiting to be unleashed. Go forward. Slay your dragons. And vanquish the Common and Hidden Forces of the Enemy.

My final challenge for you is to create your Alter Ego, cross the threshold, and reveal your Superpowers to the world.

Your mission begins now . . .

ACKNOWLEDGMENTS

Writing a book is the hardest professional dragon I've ever had to slay and more rewarding than I could've imagined. It took fifteen years of poking, prodding, and pushing from clients, friends, and peers to finally get this book into your hands. And none of this would've happened without my greatest ally, my wife, Valerie. Your late-night edits, your extra research, and your complete faith that I could pull it off gave me extra superpowers to slay the dragon. Whatever happens with this book, I've won, because I've got you with me in the foxhole.

To my children, Molly, Sophie, and Charlie, thanks for reminding me every day the power of playing with alter egos. You're the best inspiration I could ever have. You help me keep "the main thing, the main thing."

Without winning the golden ticket of getting two phenomenal parents, who knows where life would've led me. But it most definitely wouldn't have been to this opportunity of thanking you for teaching me lessons about what it means to be hardworking, honest, and a good dad. You're my first heroes. Even though you don't know how to explain what I do to others, maybe this book will make it easier.

To my siblings, Ross, Ryan, and Kerri—you all helped shape this book in some way, mostly because I wouldn't be me without you.

Without the guidance, friendship, and support of my three greatest mentors, my career in sports and business wouldn't have happened. You've all passed on, but you need to be acknowledged for your tremendous contributions to my life. Grant Henderson, you're the greatest teacher and coach I ever had. Jim Rohn, you gave me the encouragement I needed when I was just starting out. And Harvey Dorfman, you're the greatest mental-game coach that ever lived. You took a chance on me and opened up more doors than anyone. Thank you!

Mike Sainchuk, you're the brother I got to choose. Thanks for your friendship.

To get a book out of someone is a feat accomplished by many hands. Tucker Max, it all started when we met and you said, "You're an idiot if you don't write this book." You were right, and thank you for the amazing team you have at Scribe. Amanda Ibey, you were the most patient copilot on this book. You're a master at the craft but an even better person. Thank you!

To my agents at FolioLit, Scott Hoffman and Steve Troha, you guys crushed it for me. Your expertise is beyond compare and I was lucky you jumped on this book four minutes into our initial meeting.

To my editor at Harper Business, Eric Nelson, somehow you turned me into a writer. Thanks for pushing me to make the book what it became. Now I know why you're one of the most respected editors in publishing. Eternally grateful.

Without my clients—the athletes, entrepreneurs, and business pro's I've been able to work with and be inspired by over the years—this book wouldn't have the stories it needed. Thanks for persevering and getting on the field every day.

To my team, you helped keep the ship sailing while this book took shape. Karen Baglio, thanks for all your efforts. You're a champ!

Navigating life would be hard without my crew of close friends, Gary Nealon, Glenn Ormsby, Luke Kobiolke, Jordan McIntyre, Jayson Gaignard, Dan Martell, Rob Kosberg, Kevin Hutto, Chris Winfield, Jonathan Fields, Ryan Lee, Taki Moore, and Sean Finter. I couldn't be luckier than to have all of you as friends.

And finally, thank you to the family and people I've known in the four key places I've lived that shaped me: my small farm communities of Schuler and Medicine Hat, Alberta; the amazing people of Edmonton, Alberta; and the ambitious hard-charging people of New York City.

And finally, thank *you*. I hope the book impacts you like the ideas within it have impacted thousands of others.

NOTES

Chapter 2: The Origin of Alter Egos

1. *Collins English Dictionary—Complete and Unabridged*, 10th ed. (London: William Collins, 2009), retrieved January 13, 2013.
2. *The Oprah Winfrey Show*, episode 516, "How a Pair of Oprah's Shoes Changed One Woman's Life," aired September 19, 2015, http://www.oprah.com/own-where-are-they-now/how-a-pair-of-oprahs-shoes-changed-one-womans-life-video#ixzz5Kh8Czoef.
3. M. J. Brown, E. Henriquez, and J. Groscup, "The Effects of Eyeglasses and Race on Juror Decisions Involving a Violent Crime," *American Journal of Forensic Psychology* 26, no. 2 (2008): 25–43.
4. Mike Vilensky, "Report: People Wearing Glasses Seem Like People You Can Trust," *New York* magazine, February 13, 2011, http://nymag.com/daily/intelligencer/2011/02/nerd_defense.html.
5. The *Legacy of a Dream* exhibition in Concourse E at the Atlanta-Hartsfield Airport in conjunction with the King Center. One of the display cases contains the nonprescription glasses King wore to make himself feel more distinguished.

Chapter 3: The Power of the Alter Ego Effect

1. Beyoncé interview, September 2003.
2. Beyoncé, *Marie Claire* interview, October 2008.
3. Ibid.
4. Beyoncé, press statement, 2008.
5. Stephanie M. Carlson, "The Batman Effect: What My Research Shows About Pretend Play and Executive Functioning," Understood, May 30, 2016, https://www.understood.org/en/community-events/blogs/expert-corner/2016/05/30/the-batman-effect-what-my-research-shows-about-pretend-play-and-executive-functioning.
6. Ibid.
7. Rachel E. White, Emily O. Prager, Catherine Schaefer, Ethan Kross, Angela L. Duckworth, and Stephanie M. Carlson, "The 'Batman Effect': Improving Perseverance in Young Children," *Child Development*,

December 16, 2016, https://onlinelibrary.wiley.com/doi/full/10.1111
/cdev.12695.

8. Ibid.

9. Frode Stenseng, Jostein Rise, and Pål Kraft, "Activity Engagement as
Escape from Self: The Role of Self-Suppression and Self-Expansion,"
Leisure Sciences 34, no. 1 (2012): 19–38.

10. Frode Stenseng, Jostein Rise, and Pål Kraft, "The Dark Side of Leisure:
Obsessive Passion and Its Covariates and Outcomes," *Leisure Studies* 30,
no. 1 (2011): 49–62; and Frode Stenseng, "The Two Faces of Leisure
Activity Engagement: Harmonious and Obsessive Passion in Relation to
Intrapersonal Conflict and Life Domain Outcomes," *Leisure Sciences* 30,
no. 5 (2008): 465–81.

11. Ryan M. Niemiec, "VIA Character Strengths: Research and Practice
(The First 10 Years)," in Hans Henrik Knoop and Antonella Delle Fave,
eds., *Well-Being and Cultures* (Springer Netherlands, 2013).

12. Michael Shurtleff, *Audition* (New York: Bantam Books, 1978), 5.

13. Oliver James, *Upping Your Ziggy* (London: Karnac Books, 2016), xii.

14. Ibid.

15. Ibid.

Chapter 6: The Hidden Forces of the Enemy

1. Carl Richards, "Learning to Deal with the Imposter Syndrome," *New
York Times*, October 26, 2015, https://www.nytimes.com/2015/10/26
/your-money/learning-to-deal-with-the-impostor-syndrome.html.

Chapter 8: The Power of Your Story

1. Lisa Kron, *Wired for Story* (New York: Ten Speed Press, 2015), 8.

2. Seth Godin, *All Marketers Are Liars* (New York: Penguin, 2005), 3.

3. Ibid., 2.

4. Ibid., 3.

Chapter 9: Choosing Your Extraordinary World

1. Jim Carrey's commencement address at the 2014 MUM graduation, May
24, 2014, https://www.youtube.com/watch?v=V80-gPkpH6M.

2. Ibid.

3. Matt Mullin, "Ajayi Compares 'Jay Train' Persona to Brian Dawkins'
'Weapon X' Alter Ego," *Philly Voice,* January 10, 2018, http://www

.phillyvoice.com/ajayi-compares-jay-train-persona-brian-dawkins-weapon
-x-alter-ego/.

4. Steven Kotler, "Flow States and Creativity," *Psychology Today*, February
25, 2014, https://www.psychologytoday.com/us/blog/the-playing
-field/201402/flow-states-and-creativity.

5. Ibid.

6. Frode Stenseng, Jostein Rise, and Pål Kraft, "Activity Engagement as
Escape from Self: The Role of Self-Suppression and Self-Expansion,"
Leisure Sciences 34, no. 1 (2012): 19–38.

Chapter 10: The Power of a Mission

1. Roy F. Baumeister, "Some Key Differences between a Happy Life and a
Meaningful Life," *Journal of Positive Psychology* 8, no. 6 (2013).

2. Barbara Fredrickson and Steven W. Cole, National Academy of Sciences,
July 29, 2013.

3. Steven Pinker, *How the Mind Works* (New York: Norton, 1997), 373.

4. Taiichi Ohno, "Ask 'Why' Five Times About Every Matter," Toyota,
March 2006, http://www.toyota-global.com/company/toyota_traditions
/quality/mar_apr_2006.html.

5. Ethan Kross and Özlem Ayduk, "Making Meaning Out of Negative Experiences by Self-Distancing," *Current Directions in Psychological Science*
20, no. 3 (2011): 187–91.

Chapter 13: The Heroic Origin Story

1. Ibid.

2. Alison Flood, "JK Rowling Says She Received 'Loads' of Rejections Before Harry Potter Success," *Guardian*, March 24, 2015, https://www
.theguardian.com/books/2015/mar/24/jk-rowling-tells-fans-twitter
-loads-rejections-before-harry-potter-success.

3. Ibid.

4. Ibid.

Chapter 14: Activating Your Alter Ego with a Totem or Artifact

1. Joe Wright, dir., *Darkest Hour*, 2017, Perfect World Pictures.

2. Hajo Adam and Adam D. Galinsky, "Enclothed Cognition," *Journal of
Experimental Social Psychology* 48, no. 4 (July 2012): 918–25.

3. Ibid.

Chapter 16: Mindsets, Missions, Quests, and Adventures

1. Robert Stein, "Do You Want to See Her?" *American Heritage* 56, no. 5 (2005).
2. Frode Stenseng, Jostein Rise, and Pål Kraft, "Activity Engagement as Escape from Self: The Role of Self-Suppression and Self-Expansion," *Leisure Sciences* 34, no. 1 (2012): 19–38.
3. Hajo Adam and Adam D. Galinsky, "Enclothed Cognition," *Journal of Experimental Social Psychology* 48, no. 4 (July 2012): 918–25.
4. Ryan M. Niemiec, "VIA Character Strengths: Research and Practice (The First 10 Years)," in Hans Henrik Knoop and Antonella Delle Fave, eds., *Well-Being and Cultures* (Springer Netherlands, 2013).
5. Bethany E. Kok and Barbara L. Fredrickson, "Upward Spirals of the Heart: Autonomic Flexibility, as Indexed by Vagal Tone, Reciprocally and Prospectively Predicts Positive Emotions and Social Connectedness," *Biological Psychology* 85, no. 3 (2010): 432–36.
6. Joseph Campbell, *The Hero with a Thousand Faces* (Princeton, NJ: Princeton University Press, 1949), 23.
7. George Lucas interview, National Arts Club, 1985.
8. Ibid.

INDEX

ABOUT THE AUTHOR

Todd Herman is a high-performance coach and mental game strategist for ambitious entrepreneurs, athletes, and leaders who want to achieve wildly outrageous goals. He's helped clients reach the Olympic podium, build multimillion-dollar companies, and establish brands that have become internationally known. He's owned his sports science training company for over twenty years, and his signature performance system, the 90 Day Year, has been named the world's top leadership and skill development program—twice! He dodges taxis in New York City where he lives with his wife, Valerie; two girls, Molly and Sophie; and one little guy, Charlie. He is currently the world's worst ukulele player, but working on it.

Visit AlterEgoEffect.com for more resources and to share your epic story with others.